1000

Last of the Summer Wine Facts

Ben Wharton

Contents

Introduction

With its gentle humour, bumbling escapades, and endearing charm, Last of the Summer Wine has become a cultural phenomenon around the globe.

Step into the picturesque Yorkshire countryside and prepare for a delightful exploration of this long-running and iconic sitcom. This fact book is a treasure trove of fascinating trivia about the show that captured the hearts of millions.

So grab a cup of tea and a sticky bun, sit back, and immerse yourself in 1000 facts all about one of television's most beloved shows.

1000 Last of the Summer Wine Facts

(1) The first ever Summer Wine episode, Of Funerals and Fish, went out in January 1973 as part of the Comedy Playhouse - a one-off series of comic anthologies.

Many of these one-off Comedy Playhouse specials went onto to become sitcoms - not only Summer Wine but also Steptoe and Son, Till Death Us Do Part, Up Pompeii!, Not in Front of the Children, The Liver Birds, and Are You Being Served?

(2) Holmfirth was chosen as the main location for Last of the Summer Wine when Barry Took made a programme about Working Men's Clubs at nearby Burnlee WMC. When producer James Gilbert was looking for a location for an episode of Comedy Playhouse, Barry Took suggested Holmfirth.

(3) Holmfirth is a small town located in the Holme Valley, within the county of West Yorkshire. It is situated roughly 6 miles south of Huddersfield and 13 miles northeast of Glossop. Holmfirth is known for its picturesque surroundings, with the Peak District National Park to the south and scenic countryside all around.

(4) Last of the Summer Wine writer Roy Clarke was certainly prone to a bit of (largely enjoyable) recycling when it came to his characters. Auntie Wainwright in Summer Wine is a miser with a little shop who can sell anything to anyone - even if they don't actually want anything. She is clearly patterned after Ronnie Barker's parsimonious shopkeeper Arkwright in Roy's Open All Hours.

Hobo in the last embers of Summer Wine is full of (highly dubious and unlikely) tales about his exploits as a spy and action man. Hobo plainly has a lot of similarities with Foggy Dewhurst (who was also fond of tall tales about his heroic deeds). Jean Alexander was able to elevate her material and make Auntie Wainwright a distinctive and amusing character but the same can't quite be said of Russ Abbot as Hobo. Hobo came across as rehash of Foggy with a slab of Russ's Basildon Bond character thrown in.

Another piece of Roy's recycling came when Alvin Smedley moved into Compo's house and Brian Murphy was put through some of Compo's old comic paces in his comedic sparring with Nora Batty. Thora Hird's Edie in Summer Wine has some similarities with Roy Clarke's Hyacinth Bucket in Keeping Up Appearances in that both characters like to give the impression to neighbours they are of a higher class. Edie always puts on a posh voice when she calls Wesley into the house. On the whole though, Edie is far less insufferable than Hyacinth! You could say too there is some plot/scenario recycling in that Wally Batty was forever trying to escape from Nora and get out of the house. Howard later had a similar fate to Wally in that he too was always trying to leave the house and escape from his formidable wife - who in this case was obviously Pearl. Their motivations were different though in that Wally simply wanted to see his pigeons or get a pint. Howard on the other hand was motivated by his endless desire to secretly meet up with Marina.

(5) Norman Clegg was a bit more confident and abrasive at the start of the show compared to the meeker Cleggy of later seasons. This was probably a natural consequence of Peter Sallis growing into the character and adapting it somewhat - alongside the changes made by Roy Clarke. It was also, you could argue, a consequence of Cleggy getting older too.

(6) It is plainly no coincidence that Foggy's real name is Walter. Walter Mitty is a fictional character created by writer James Thurber. He first appeared in Thurber's 1939 short story

The Secret Life of Walter Mitty. Mitty is a daydreamer who often escapes into elaborate fantasies to compensate for his relatively dull and mundane life. In his daydreams, he assumes various heroic personas and engages in exciting adventures, contrasting with his rather subservient and meek real-life persona.

(7) Compo's real name is William Simmonite. The nickname 'Compo' comes from the fact that Compo is on unemployment compensation - which explains why he never has a job. To be honest, Compo is probably unemployable. It is difficult to see him lasting very long in a job!

(8) The early episodes of Summer Wine were built much more around long dialogue scenes with the main trio - usually in the library and the pub. It was only in later series where more slapstick and action comedy (for want of a better phrase) came in on a regular basis and there would be some elaborate comic stunt in which poor Compo was usually the stuntman.

(9) Keith Clifford (as Billy) was the first actor in a Summer Wine 'main trio' who came from Yorkshire in real life. Bill Owen and Peter Sallis were born in London, Brian Wilde was from Lancashire, Michael Aldridge was born in Somerset, and Michael Bates was born in India to parents from Cheshire.

(10) Ivy's catchphrase "What the blood and stomach pills!" comes from sugar coated 'blood and stomach pills' you used to be able to buy from chemists.

(11) If an episode of Last of the Summer Wine was found to be running short, Roy Clarke would hastily write an extra scene and fax it to the set!

(12) According to Compo's passport in the special episode Last Post and Pigeon, Compo was born in 1923. This means that Compo was only about 49 when Last of the Summer

Wine first began! Bill Owen was born in 1914 so he was older than the character in real life.

(13) Wesley Pegden, played by Gordon Wharmby, first appeared in the 1982 episode Car and Garter in a cameo role. He returned in The Loxley Lozenge and Who's Looking After The Cafe Then?. The 1985 feature-length Christmas special Uncle of the Bride established Wesley as the husband of Edie and he became a beloved regular character. No episode was quite complete without a trip to Wesley's exploding shed - where he was usually involved in some noisy operation on some old car or engine he'd retrieved. Wesley often played an important role in the plots as the main trio would usually enlist Wesley's mechanical skills to facilitate whatever crackpot scheme they (and by 'they' we mean Foggy and Seymour!) had come up with that week. Wesley could also be relied upon to appear out of nowhere in the countryside and give the main trio a lift back to town!

(14) The women having coffee and a gossip at Edie's became a regular fixture in the show. Edie's catchphrase ("Drink your coffee!") and the battle over who would get the eclair or cream cake (the losers had to make do with a biscuit) were staples of these scenes. The first 'ladies coffee morning' scene in the show was in the 1988 episode The Experiment.

(15) Michael Bates, who played Blamire, left Summer Wine when he was diagnosed with cancer in 1975 (though he did still appear in It Ain't Half Hot Mum). Sadly, he died in 1978. In the first episode after Michael Bates left, Cleggy reads a letter from Blamire asking that they look after his friend Foggy Dewhurst. Blamire leaving is explained in the show by him learning that an old flame had been widowed. Blamire clearly decided to go and pursue this old flame.

(16) The last ever line by anyone in Last of the Summer Wine is Cleggy saying "Did I lock the door?" at the end of the last

episode. It seems appropriate that Cleggy had the last word and even more appropriate that he was worrying about something!

(17) Roy Clarke said he used to give his best lines to Peter Sallis because Cleggy was his favourite character.

(18) John Comer appeared in 46 episodes of Last of the Summer Wine from 1973 to 1983 as Sid - the owner of the cafe and husband of Ivy. Comer sadly died of throat cancer in 1984. His last appearance in the show was in the Christmas film Getting Sam Home. Comer's lines as Sid were dubbed by Tony Melody because the cancer had affected his ability to speak. John Comer had an eclectic and interesting career aside from Summer Wine. He was in a variety double act on the stage and appeared in shows like Coronation Street and The Avengers. He was in a number of films too - including an uncredited role in the cult horror sequel Dr Phibes Rises Again. Sid was a very likeable character so it was a great loss to the show when John Comer passed away. What was fun about Sid too is that he was a 'partner in crime' to the main trio in that they confided in him and he usually tried to help them.

(19) For the record, Compo only went down a hill in a bath once in Last of the Summer Wine. Casual retrospectives of the show by those who haven't really watched much of it seem to think this happened every single week!

(20) Auntie Wainwright, the miserly and cunning owner of the local bric-a-brac shop, made her first appearance in 1988 Christmas Special Crums and then returned again for another Christmas special. Auntie Wainwright became a regular character in 1992. Jean Alexander was already something of a national treasure thanks to her long stint in Coronation Street as the legendary Hilda Ogden. Jean was not only a brilliant actor but also had a natural gift for comedy. She appeared in

168 episodes of Summer Wine and stayed until the end of the show. The characters in the show making a trip to Auntie Wainwright's shop, where they would inevitably be sold some random useless item that they didn't even want in the first place, became a fixture of Summer Wine. Cleggy in particular has a deep fear of Auntie Wainwright! It is rather odd by the way that when the characters are in need of something they always go to Auntie Wainwright. You'd think this was the only shop in Yorkshire!

(21) Elegy for Fallen Wellies, Surprise at Throstlenest, and Just a Small Funeral were written in quick order to account for Bill Owen's death. These three episodes, which deal with Compo's death and funeral, contain some of Roy Clarke's best writing. Although these episodes still have humour they are also surprisingly moving at times and there is some terrific 'straight' acting by the cast in some scenes - especially Peter Sallis as Cleggy. Compo was Cleggy's best friend for decades so he feels the loss more than anyone.

(22) Last of the Summer Wine became more of an ensemble piece as it went on with a larger collection of characters than the early years. It is sometimes assumed this was a consequence of the core characters getting older and lessening their workload but Roy Clarke said making the cast larger was something he decided to do simply because it gave him more scope with his scripts. Roy also said that he enjoyed all the supporting characters they'd created so he wanted to make them a permanent part of the show and use them more.

(23) Roy Clarke said the Summer Wine rarely got a good review once the audience figures got massive. The more popular the show became the sniffier the reviews from critics got.

(24) Seymour, Edie, Glenda and Barry made their first appearances in the 1986 New Year special Uncle of the Bride.

We learn in this episode that Foggy has moved to Bridlington to take over an egg painting business. Just over 18 million people watched Uncle of the Bride when it was first broadcast. Viewing figures like that would be impossible today. Uncle of the Bride was broadcast at a time when there were four television channels and the internet and streaming didn't exist. There wasn't much else to watch!

(25) In 1988, a prequel show titled First of the Summer Wine began on the BBC. The show was set in 1939 and revolved around the familiar Summer Wine characters - only in their younger years. David Fenwick played Cleggy, Paul Wyett was Compo, and Richard Lumsden was Foggy. We also meet younger versions of Wally and Nora. Paul McLain played Seymour - which didn't make much sense in continuity terms because in Last of the Summer the characters Compo and Clegg don't seem to know Seymour when they first meet him! Peter Sallis played the father of Clegg in First of the Summer Wine. First of the Summer Wine ran to two series in the end. It was quite pleasant but it didn't really catch on or become a big hit. The fact that it was a period show and so quite expensive to make (what with the costumes and 1930s trappings) was probably the reason why it didn't last very long.

(26) After the death of John Comer as Sid, Jonathan Linsley joined the cast in 1984 as Sid and Ivy's hulking nephew 'Crusher' Milburn. Crusher was a gentle giant who worked at the cafe for Ivy. Jonathan Linsley left the show in 1987 because he lost about fourteen stone in weight and was almost unrecognisable compared to how he looked as Crusher. Linsley said that the BBC were rather vague about whether Crusher would be in any new episodes so he decided to move on with his career and lose some weight for health reasons. The BBC then said that they wanted him back but by now it was too late because he had lost half his body weight! Jonathan said it was probably for the best that he left the show because he probably would have been typecast had he played

Crusher for too long. He later appeared in two Pirates of the Caribbean movies. Around the time that he left Summer Wine, Jonathan appeared in commercials for John Smith's Yorkshire Bitter with Jane Freeman. Jonathan said he made a lot more money doing these commercials than he did on Summer Wine!

(27) Danny O'Dea, born Peter Anthony Joseph Daniel Wrenshall in 1911, played Eli in Last of the Summer Wine from 1986 to 2002. Eli was essentially a Yorkshire version of Mr Magoo and would have a little comic cameo in most episodes. The jaunty music cue would herald a comic vignette of short-sighted capers featuring Eli. Eli never really featured in the plots of the episodes - though occasionally the main trio would try to enlist his help in some task without much success.

Danny O'Dea was from the music hall tradition and worked with many big names in comedy. He did pantomimes and his other credits include All Creatures Great and Small and Victoria Wood. Danny O'Dea passed away in 2002. Although the deaths of actors were usually written into the show (in that their characters would become past tense in the show - indicating that they had passed in Summer Wine) this was not done to explain why Eli was no longer in the show. This is presumably because Eli was a cameo player and not involved in many scenes or the plots. Eli was originally brought into the show as a friend of Wally Batty but stayed on after the death of Joe Gladwin.

(28) Producer and director Alan J W Bell had what you might describe as a strained relationship with the BBC in the last few years of the show. Alan complained that the BBC were constantly cutting the budget on Summer Wine and had been trying to get rid of the show for years.

(29) Pearl, Howard, and Marina were first introduced in the

Summer Wine play produced for the stage. Bill Owen and Peter Sallis reprised their roles as Compo and Clegg but Brian Wilde declined to take part. Howard was initially played by Kenneth Waller (best known as the grumpy Grandad in the sitcom Bread) while Pearl was played by a local actress. Robert Fyfe replaced Waller in the role of Howard and Juliette Kaplan took the role of Pearl. These two actors were then cast as Howard and Peal in the television show and stayed until the end - appearing in hundreds of episodes.

(30) Juliette Kaplan had never even heard of Last of the Summer Wine when she was cast in the stage show as Pearl!

(31) Jean Fergusson as Marina was another person who went into the television show from the stage play. Jean Fergusson was a prolific stage actress and combined Summer Wine with touring in plays. Jean won many plaudits for her role as Hylda Baker in the play She Knows, You Know.

(32) Roy Clarke said that Last of the Summer Wine was a 'love letter to the past'. The characters in the show and the place they live frequently seem largely untouched by the modern world.

(33) Stephen Lewis as Smiler made his first appearance in Summer Wine in the series ten episode That Certain Smile. Smiler's nickname is not used in this episode. His real name is Clem Hemmingway. In the episode, the trio try to sneak Smiler's dog to his hospital room to cheer him up. Smiler would later return and become a regular character. He was a lollipop man, a lodger with Nora Batty, and then worked for Auntie Wainwright. I'm not which is worse - lodging with Nora or working for Auntie Wainwright!

Stephen Lewis was obviously most famous for playing the comical and long suffering jobsworth Inspector Cyril "Blakey" Blake in On the Buses. Stephen Lewis brought a lot of Blakey's lugubrious exasperation to the part of the world weary Smiler. Stephen Lewis left Summer Wine after series twenty-eight due to ill health. Tom Simmonite later mentions that Smiler just 'disappeared'.

(34) Mike Grady appeared in 161 episodes of Last of the Summer Wine as the mild mannered building society employee Barry Wilkinson. Barry was introduced in the feature length special Uncle of the Bride in 1986. Mike left the show in 1990 for six years before returning in 1996 and staying until the end. Mike's hiatus was to do other acting work. Mike Grady has many acting credits to his name. He has been in films like The Return of the Pink Panther, Carry On Loving, and Sherlock Holmes: A Game of Shadows. Mike was in his fifties when he returned to Summer Wine for his second stint but the other characters still call him 'lad'! Barry is quite rare in Summer Wine in that he is a husband but has a happy marriage and a friendly, gentle wife who is kind to him!

(35) Bill Owen once said of Compo - "I am not at all like him but we probably share a zest for living."

(36) Yvette Fielding, later best known as the presenter of the paranormal investigation show Most Haunted, appeared in the 1988 Christmas special as Crusher's girlfriend Fran.

(37) Roy Clarke said that health and safety regulations eventually put a stop to the crazy stunts they used to do on Last of the Summer Wine!

(38) Barnpot is a northern slang word for someone who is a bit daft. Cleggy is fond of this word - especially in relation to Foggy!

(39) In the scenes where Compo gets a bucket of water poured over his head by Nora Batty, Bill Owen always insisted on doing this himself rather than use a double. Bill thought it was funnier if the viewers saw it was really him (Compo) getting drenched.

(40) Mike Grady said that when he was in Summer Wine he never got to know Bill Owen or Brian Wilde very well because neither of them were very social people and they tended to keep themselves to themselves. Mike said they were both very nice but just quite private and shy men in real life.

(41) Norman Clegg was a Co-op lino (linoleum) salesman. Cleggy is the first to admit that this wasn't the most exciting job in the world!

(42) The Robin Hood obsessed Billy Hardcastle made his first appearance in the 1999 episode How Errol Flynn Discovered the Secret Scar of Nora Batty. After a couple more guest spots, Billy became a regular in the 22nd series. Billy essentially replaced Compo in the end and the new main trio became Cleggy, Truly, and Billy for a time. Billy was played by Keith Clifford. After appearing in 66 episodes of Summer Wine, Keith decided to leave the show in 2006 so that he could do other acting work. In 2007 he took a role in Coronation Street - a show in which he'd played other characters in the past.

(43) The character of Hobbo Hobdyke, played by Russ Abbot, is a former milkman who believes he was a Jason Bourne type spy who worked for MI5 but then had many of his memories wiped. Foggy Dewhurst (on whom Hobo is clearly based) had a degree of plausibility in that he was romantic and nostalgic about his time in the forces and so had embellished that period in his imagination. We get the impression that Foggy has told so many tall tales about his army career that he actually believes them. Hobo on the other hand is just a bit too silly and implausible.

The character of Hobo, for some fans, did not really work in the twilight of Summer Wine. Besides the fact that Hobo felt like a slightly tiresome rehash of Foggy, one of the other problems is that Russ Abbot becomes the dominant comic character in the new trio and so Brian Murphy in particular, who was quite funny as Alvin in previous series, is too often now reduced to simply just standing there reacting to whatever Russ Abbot is doing. The character of Alvin is plainly hobbled by this new dynamic. One can sort of understand the strategy in that the show was seeking to replicate past chemistry by having Alvin and Entwistle paired with a Walter Mitty type 'leader' (as Foggy was) but it didn't really work terribly well. The memorable Foggy/Cleggy/Compo dynamic and chemistry was simply impossible to replicate with different actors.

(44) Juliette Kaplan looked nothing like Pearl in real life. Occasionally in the show they have Pearl shed her 'battleaxe' outfit and look more glamorous or conventional. In these scenes we see that Howard is always a trifle confused and disturbed to see that his wife is actually quite attractive when she wants to be!

(45) The episode titled When You take a Good Bite, Yorkshire Tastes Terrible was a personal favourite of Roy Clarke and Peter Sallis. This is a very enjoyable episode because Cleggy, usually the last person to volunteer for anything, decides to complete a series of challenges in memory of an old friend who has recently died. When You take a Good Bite, Yorkshire Tastes Terrible is a very sweet episode. It was rather bittersweet one behind the scenes too because it marked the last ever appearance in the show of Wally Batty. Joe Gladwin passed away a few weeks before this episode was broadcast.

(46) Despite being the world's longest running sitcom, Summer Wine did not get a special farewell episode. "I returned home and found an email which said that there would be no filming of the series the following year," said Alan J W Bell. "At first I thought it was a joke, for I had

discussed my strategy with the Head of Comedy, but it was true."

(47) Roy Clarke, by contrast, said the end of the show was not a surprise to him nor even a disappointment. "A lot of the stories questioned if I had any bad feeling toward the BBC. I'm a freelance – who could complain about a company that has given you 40 years of work? All good things must come to an end is a cliche but it's true. The end was bound to happen and I've got great respect and gratitude for the Beeb for supporting us all these years. I've also got to thank the audience for being so faithful. We've always had respectable viewing figures and that's because of them; they are the reason it's lasted so long. The timing is right because we're all getting so doddery!"

(48) Roy Clarke said he was very surprised to be asked to write a script for the Comedy Playhouse (which obviously led to Summer Wine becoming a series) because at the time he didn't think of himself as a comedy writer.

(49) Brian Wilde as Foggy left Last of the Summer Wine in 1985 - though he would of course return in 1990. It is believed that, when Brian Wilde first started to hint he might be leaving the show, Fulton Mackay, best known of course for starring in Porridge (alongside Wilde), was contacted about the possibility of replacing Wilde in Last of the Summer Wine. One can certainly imagine Mackay, who was a fine comic actor and good at playing somewhat pompous characters, making a good foil for Compo and Clegg. Sadly though, Fulton Mackay died of cancer in 1987 so if he had been cast ill health would have made his tenure in Summer Wine very short.

(50) Kathy Staff appeared in 243 episodes of Last of the Summer Wine as the formidable broom wielding Nora Batty. Kathy decided to leave the show when Bill Owen died because she said it wouldn't be the same but she was persuaded to come back. Sadly, Kathy died a few years before the show ended. Nora's absence in the show was explained by her looking after relatives in Australia. Kathy Staff was a very gentle woman in real life so it took a good costume and some even better acting to turn her into the stern Nora.

(51) Kathy Staff was best known for Nora Batty but she actually appeared in more episodes of the soap opera Crossroads than she did Summer Wine. Kathy was in 324 episodes of Crossroads as Doris Luke.

(52) One thing that hasn't aged well in some of the Summer Wine episodes is the use of back projection when the characters are in a car - or sometimes even when Compo is involved in a stunt. Back projection tends to look very fake so it takes us out the scene. Thankfully though they didn't do this all the time.

(53) Peter Sallis had known Michael Bates for 20 years before they played Cleggy and Blamire in the early series of Summer Wine. The two had appeared in a couple of plays together. Peter said that Michael Bates was a perfectionist who liked to keep doing scenes until they were perfect.

(54) Robert Fyfe, who played Howard, was from Scotland in real life. You wouldn't know it though because his Yorkshire accent in the show is pretty good. The same can be said of Bill Owen - who was a southerner in real life. Peter Sallis confessed that he never really made a serious attempt to do a strong Yorkshire accent as Cleggy - lest it should come off wrong. Peter slips into his own accent at times on the show, especially later on, but you don't really notice much.

(55) There is rarely any car traffic in Last of the Summer Wine - especially on the country roads the main trio walk. This is because roads were usually blocked off and closed for shooting. It obviously would have been nigh on impossible to shoot scenes if there was a chance of a car or lorry suddenly thundering past. You often see traffic off in the distance though.

(56) Viewers who got into Summer Wine through repeats on freeview are doubtless a bit confused as to why Foggy is suddenly gone in the episode Beware of the Oglethorpe and has been replaced by Herbert "Truly" Truelove. Why is Foggy's absence not mentioned at all? Well, this was addressed in the 1997 Christmas special There Goes the Groom. In this episode we meet Truly for the first time and Foggy proposes marriage to a post lady in Blackpool - thus explaining why the character has left the show. Brian Wilde wasn't actually in this episode and a drunken Foggy was depicted by a body double (Colin Harris).

The freeview repeats of Summer Wine tend not to show the (longer) Christmas specials (at least not in order with the traditional episodes) so a lot of Summer Wine fans who only watched the repeats on freeview may have missed the Christmas special which explains what happened to Foggy. Truly was only supposed to appear in this Christmas special but Brian Wilde decided not to return due to poor health so Frank Thornton as Truly replaced Foggy in series nineteen. It was actually Brian Wilde who suggested Thornton as his replacement in the Christmas special (which Wilde did not appear due to a scheduling problem and a bad leg) but Thornton went from being a temporary replacement to a permanent one.

(57) The character of Truly seemed a bit ill-defined at first because Frank Thornton was plainly having to play scripts that were written for Brian Wilde's Foggy. Frank Thornton was eventually able to put his own stamp on Truly. What was especially good about Frank Thornton's performance was the way he crafted a very believable and warm friendship

between Cleggy and Truly. This was most in evidence during the poignant episodes that dealt with Compo's death. In these episodes the kind and loyal Truly offers invaluable support to the distraught Cleggy.

(58) Circa 2014, there was an attempt to do a Last of the Summer Wine spin-off show featuring Ken Kitson as PC Cooper and Louis Emerick as PC Walsh - the two somewhat lazy and timid police officers who frequently popped up in Last of the Summer Wine. The two officers were usually parked in some remote rural spot to avoid doing any police work but inevitably chanced upon some crackpot 'barnpottery' which had abounded from the main trio of characters. A pilot of Cooper and Walsh was released in 2014 over the go-fund-me website. It did not though result in a full series. Tony Capstick also played the 'second police officer' alongside Kitson. Tony Captstick died in 2003. In the show his departure is explained by his character having been transferred to the police in Huddersfield.

(59) There is a speculative fan theory that Pearl is related to Cleggy's late wife Edith. This theory therefore explains why Pearl seems to have a soft spot for Cleggy. It is purely a fan theory though. Another explanation for why Marina seems to like Clegg ("Norman Clegg that was!") is Cleggy's revelation that he was once trapped in a lift with Marina and she had to comfort him. Despite this though, Clegg is plainly terrified of Marina!

(60) Norman Clegg was married to Edith from 1940 to 1971. Edith is only mentioned once by name in Summer Wine although Cleggy does make a number of references to his marriage throughout the show. Given that Cleggy seems to be terrified of women it is hard to believe that he had a wife! We get the impression, from the occasional references to her, that Edith probably wasn't the biggest barrel of laughs and Cleggy was probably a bit under the thumb. However, there are also

some very subtle hints that Clegg misses his wife.

(61) Trevor Bannister played Toby Mulberry Smith in Summer Wine. Toby is the captain of the golf club and later Barry's next door neighbour. Trevor Bannister had previously played a tailor in the 1992 Summer Wine episode Who's Got Rhythm? He appeared in 24 episodes of Summer Wine and was a regular character in its last days. Trevor Bannister was a good friend of Frank Thornton because they had both obviously been prominent cast members in Are You Being Served?

(62) Roy Clarke admitted that the characters of Alvin and Billy didn't work when they were put together because they were too similar. It worked better when there was just one of them and they presented more of a contrast to the other main characters. By way of example, Billy sort of worked with with Cleggy and Truly because he was different from them - just as Compo had been. Billy complimented Cleggy and Truly but with Alvin and Billy it felt like they occupied the same comedic space to the point where they almost started to cancel one another out.

(63) After the death of Bill Owen, his son Tom Owen joined the show in 2000 as Compo's long lost son Tom Simmonite. Tom was an actor like his father and had appeared in shows like Minder and Upstairs, Downstairs. He had also previously made appearances in Summer Wine in background or guest parts. It is probably fair to say that for some fans the character of Tom Simmonite didn't quite work. Tom Simmonite was a bit of a shyster at first in the show, hiding in his allotment shed from the repo man, clowning with a puppet dog, and coming up with dubious business schemes. He and Lolly Minerva Avery (Julie T. Wallace) had a bus. Mrs Avery was a fake fortune teller. None of this stuff worked terribly well and none of it was very funny. The character of Babs Avery (Helen Turaya), Mrs Avery's niece, was deemed so unfunny and unpopular she disappeared after a few episodes. Tom

Simmonite's role in the show was gradually reduced and he became a background character who worked for Auntie Wainwright and knocked around with Smiler. At the start it was apparently the plan that Tom Simmonite would replace Compo in the main trio but they obviously didn't go through with this in the end. Tom Owen didn't have any obvious comic chemistry with Peter Sallis or Frank Thornton and he also tended to mug his lines and jokes a trifle too much in his early episodes. It was a nice idea to bring in Bill Owen's son but, ultimately, it didn't quite work as well as they might have hoped. To be fair though, Tom did get better in the show later on and had a likeable screen presence. He made a good double act with Smiler. I should point out that for some fans it was the reverse in that they preferred the first version Tom as the wheeler/dealer con-man rather than the later Tom working for Auntie Wainwright. It's all down to personal opinion really.

(64) Thora Bird played Edie in Summer Wine right up to her death in 2003. Thora was in her nineties in her last episodes so they had to use a stand in for scenes where Edie is standing up because Thora wasn't mobile anymore.

(65) When he left Summer Wine in 1985, Brian Wilde starred in a BBC sitcom called Wyatt's Watchdogs in which he played a retired soldier named Major John Wyatt who forms a Neighbourhood Watch group made up of somewhat incompetent local characters. The show was co-created by Alan J W Bell, who was of course a long running director and producer on Summer Wine. The character Brian Wilde played in Wyatt's Watchdogs had some obvious similarities with Foggy although Wyatt, on the whole, was more assertive and brave than Foggy (who always talked a good game but was usually hopeless in a confrontation). Wyatt's Watchdogs never really caught on and was axed after one series - which paved the way for Brian Wilde to return to Summer Wine when Michael Aldridge (who played Seymour) left the show to look

after his sick wife. It is said that Brian Wilde left Summer Wine in 1985 partly due to creative disagreements with Alan J W Bell but they obviously must have patched things up On Wyatt's Watchdogs because Brian returned as Foggy in 1990.

(66) Christopher Beeny joined the cast of Summer Wine in 2001 as the "Repo Man" Herman Teesdale - who was always trying to track down Tom Simmonite. The character later changed his name to Morton Beemish and cultivated a friendship with (a rather reluctant) Barry. Beemish then became a sort of lodger/skivvy for Toby Mulberry Smith. He was in 27 episodes in all. Christopher Beeny was best known for his role as Edward in Upstairs, Downstairs and also for the period sitcom In Loving Memory - in which he starred with Thora Hird.

(67) At the start of Summer Wine, Nora Batty was not intended to be a prominent or regular character but Roy Clarke liked Nora and Kathy Staff's performance so much he expanded her role in the show.

(68) The feature length special Uncle Of The Bride is the first episode in the show where it is mentioned that Sid has died.

(69) Howard must be the worst liar in Yorkshire. After hundreds of episodes being caught with Marina, in all manner of places, he still insists that he 'hardly knows the lady'!

(70) The episode Catching Digby's Donkey, which aired in March 1985, marked the first appearance of Howard, Pearl, and Marina. These characters became regulars and Howard's endless (and usually doomed) attempts to sneak away from Pearl to see Marina without being detected became a fixture in the show.

(71) Michael Bates said that he was very sad that poor health forced his character Blamire to be written out of Summer

Wine. Bates said he was touched when he saw the first episode after his departure and Cleggy reads out the letter from Blamire.

(72) Compo is clearly a man who loves his grub. He especially enjoys the puddings that Nora will occasionally make for him and also the sticky buns at Ivy's cafe.

(73) In a lot of old BBC sitcoms, when the characters go to a pub it is obvious they are in a studio set which is made to look like a pub. Summer Wine was different because they often filmed in real pubs. It must have been a bit of a palava getting the crew and camera equipment into a pub!

(74) What is especially nice about the episode Return of the Warrior (in which Foggy returns after five years away) is that the episode includes a nice scene at the start where Seymour says goodbye to Cleggy and Compo before taking up a teaching post. It makes the episode more satisfying to actually see Seymour before he leaves.

(75) There were plans for Seymour to come back to Summer Wine later and make guest appearances but sadly the health of Michael Aldridge didn't allow for this.

(76) The legendary stage and screen actress Dora Bryan first appeared in Last of the Summer Wine in 2000 as Roz Utterthwaite - the sister of Edie and Seymour. Dora appeared in 50 episodes of Summer Wine before leaving the show in 2005 due to ill health. The character of Roz was sort of replaced by June Whitfield as Nelly. Nelly was a member of the ladies coffee sessions and also a friend of Pearl. Nelly stayed in the show until the end although June Whitfield, for some reason, did not appear in the last episode. June Whitfield previously appeared in Summer Wine in 2001 playing a different character. In the 2001 Christmas Special Potts in Pole Position, June played a character named Delphi

Potts and Warren Mitchell (Alf Garnett himself) played her husband.

(77) Peter Sallis and some of the cast would often stay in a hotel near Huddersfield when they shot Summer Wine. Bill Owen, who didn't seem to like hotels much, would rent a cottage.

(78) You can see a photograph of Edie in Glenda and Barry's house in the last three series of Summer Wine. In the late 1990s episodes, Glenda has a photograph of Seymour in her house.

(79) In his early appearances in Summer Wine, Wesley Pegden is shown to be fond of listening to loud rock music when he is driving. This is clearly something that Edie would definitely not allow him to do at home!

(80) It was Juliette Kaplan's idea for Pearl to always wear something on her head - like a beret. This is because the wig they gave Juliette kept flapping in the wind.

(81) The classic Getting Sam Home special episode was based on a Summer Wine novel Roy Clarke had written in 1974. In the novel Blamire is one of the characters. Foggy obviously replaced Blamire in the film.

(82) Compo has a rather large extended family and we saw quite a lot of his relatives in early series. They stopped doing this at some point.

(83) Alan J W Bell said it was quite a major task scouting the locations in the countryside for Summer Wine. He said the most annoying thing, which happened occasionally, was finding that some other production crew was in the area shooting in more or less the same place!

(84) We never do find out in the show what was in Compo's matchbox (which would so alarm anyone who had a peek inside).

(85) In his initial appearances in Summer Wine, Billy Hardcastle wore a full Robin Hood costume with tights and hat. This was later modified to a more conventional green waterproof coat.

(86) Foggy's walking stick was not because Brian Wilde had a bad leg but purely an affectation for the character. Foggy is a bit pretentious and probably thinks a walking stick makes him look more distinguished.

(87) Alan J W Bell said that when he directed the show he liked to have a shot of the main trio walking in the countryside before they actually said anything. Alan said that Brian Wilde was sometimes a bit irritated by having to do all this walking!

(88) Compo is prone to breaking into song to amuse himself from time to time. Bill Owen was allowed to improvise these moments and choose the songs that Compo would sing.

(89) Peter Sallis said in an interview that Full Steam Behind was one of the episodes he loved the most. This is the classic episode where Foggy's desire to look at steam trains leads to all manner of train related trouble.

(90) When he took over as director on the show, Alan J W Bell got rid of shooting scenes at the BBC television centre and introduced more location shooting. Bell would show the episodes to a live audience in a theatre and their laughter would be used over the shows. Alan was always irritated when Summer Wine was accused of having fake canned laughter because this wasn't true. One clever and pleasant thing Alan did during the live screenings too was to get

Summer Wine cast members to appear at the start like a warm up act.

(91) Josephine Tewson joined the cast of Summer Wine in 2003 as the librarian Miss Davenport and stayed until the end - appearing in 62 episodes. Josephine also played Elizabeth "Liz" Warden in Roy Clarke's Keeping Up Appearances. In addition to a rich stage career, Josephine Tewson had a long history when it came to comedy shows. Her credits included The Two Ronnies, The Dick Emery Show, Terry and June, and Larry Grayson. She was also in the short-lived Ronnie Barker sitcom Clarence.

(92) Burt Kwouk joined the cast of Summer Wine in 2002 as Electrical Entwistle and stayed until the end. Entwistle ferried the characters around in his truck and was usually paired up with Alvin. The character dispensed amusing little comic asides. Burt Kwouk had an incredible CV and was in many big movies. He was best known though for his role as Cato, the karate chopping manservant of Inspector Clouseau, in the Pink Panther films.

(93) Mike Grady said that although Barry Wilkinson was usually depicted as the 'young' character in Summer Wine he actually had his free bus pass by the time it ended!

(94) Foggy's real name is Walter C. Dewhurst. "Foggy" comes from the English folk song Foggy Foggy Dew.

(95) Asked what his favourite era of Summer Wine was, Roy Clarke seemed to suggest he liked the early ones the best - with Blamire and the first run with Foggy.

(96) The episode titled Walking Stiff Can Make You Famous is a rarity because we see Foggy's house. Though we often go inside the homes of Cleggy and Compo we rarely got a look at where Foggy lives. There are only a couple of episodes where we see Foggy's abode.

(97) Sid's Cafe in Summer Wine used to be a fish & chip shop and was a paint store for the ironmongers next door when the BBC saw it and decided to use it as a location. It is now a real cafe that you can visit. In the show it is fairly obvious that they use the exterior but when the characters are inside the cafe they are in a studio. The cafe has nothing in front of it outside but in some episodes there is a wall right outside the window - which doesn't make any sense!

(98) In the 1970s it was common for popular television sitcoms to get a film version for cinema release. Shows like Dad's Army, On the Buses, Man About the House, Bless This House, The Likely Lads, Love Thy Neighbour, Please Sir!, Steptoe and Son, Rising Damp, Porridge, For the Love of Ada, and more all got films. However, this did not happen with Last of the Summer Wine and it seems there was never any serious consideration to doing this. One could say though that Getting Sam Home was basically the summer Wine spin-off movie and some of the feature length Christmas specials were also like Summer Wine movies. Maybe it is for the best that they didn't do a Summer Wine spin off film in the 1970s of Cleggy, Compo, and Foggy going on a package holiday to Spain or something!

(99) It is generally series five of Summer Wine where Compo performing some bizarre comical stunt (usually thanks to Foggy) became a fairly common fixture in the show.

(100) Although he had no interest in writing a special farewell episode of Summer Wine, Roy Clarke did, in a departure for him, write the last series in serial form because he suspected it would be the last.

(101) Even though Roy Clarke had a fairly good idea that Summer Wine was ending when he did he said he decided not to write a 'farewell' episode just in case someone at the BBC decided they wanted it to come back.

(102) Compo's habit of groping of Nora and Ivy is something in Summer Wine that seems dated and somewhat jarring from a modern perspective. You definitely wouldn't be able to do these scenes today. If we were to offer some mitigation we could say though that Compo does know when to draw the line and usually comes off worse in these encounters as they often result in him being the victim of a bucket of water, a broom in the face, or a tea tray being clanked over his head.

(103) Despite all their trysts and secret meetings, it seems that Howard and Marina never got any further than holding hands or riding their bikes together!

(104) Last of the Summer Wine has been praised for its refreshing depiction of old age. The characters in the show are clearly knocking on (especially in later series) but they still embrace life and find a way to have fun and be silly.

(105) John Cleese made a very brief cameo appearance in the 1993 Christmas special Welcome to Earth.

(106) One big difference between Foggy and his last replacement Truly is that Truly seems to be respected by the supporting characters in the show. Poor old Foggy never got much respect from anyone!

(107) The real location for Barry and Glenda's house exterior in Summer Wine is Green Abbey, Hade Edge, Holmfirth. The interior scenes where Barry and Glenda are inside the house were shot in a studio.

(108) Michael Bates had an amazing film career before playing Blamire in Summer Wine. He was in Hitchcock's classic suspense thriller Frenzy, Kubrick's A Clockwork Orange,

Bedazzled, Battle of Britain, Dunkirk, I'm Alright Jack, and many others. Perhaps his finest hour came when he played General Bernard Montgomery in the Oscar winning biopic Patton. Field Marshal Bernard Law Montgomery (1887–1976), known as "Monty", was the most famous British general to emerge from the war.

(109) Last of the Summer Wine is especially enjoyable because in addition to the gentle comedy it explores themes like the importance of community, the value of friendship, and the simplicity and charms of rural life. The show feels very rooted in nature - which the central trio use as a place to escape from the real world and have adventures.

(110) Jean Fergusson said that wearing Marina's flirty blouses and mini-skirts near the end of the show was a bit strange because in real life she was an old age pensioner!

(111) Roy Clarke was not happy when Bill Owen was floated as a possibility to play Compo in Last of the Summer Wine. Bill Owen was not only a Londoner but arguably best known for playing authority types. He was also quite a dapper man in real life. All in all he seemed a million miles away from Clarke's conception of Compo. However, Bill Owen was a brilliant actor and proved to be inspired casting as Compo. Roy Clarke said it was only when he watched Bill Owen in character as Compo on the screen that he realised what a gifted physical comic actor Bill was. Bill Owen brought all of the little quirks and qualities to Compo that made the character fully formed and completely unique.

(112) It was Roy Clarke who picked Peter Sallis to play Cleggy. Roy had worked with Peter before and thought he was a terrific actor. Peter Sallis was often cast as villains or unfaithful husbands so it was very clever of Roy Clarke to judge that Peter would make a likable comic actor in Summer Wine.

(113) A new series of Summer Wine was in production when Bill Owen died. Roy Clarke later said that had Bill Owen died between series the BBC might well have decided to pull the plug on the show.

(114) After 1991, the show was always shot on film. One can certainly see the difference when you watch the videotape episodes. They don't seem as lavish and nice to look at.

(115) It is a great tribute to Brian Wilde that Foggy, although a fantasist and someone who can be quite annoying and pompous at the best of times, still comes across as sympathetic - even likable. When the character came back to the show in Return of the Warrior we even feel affection when we see Foggy again.

(116) Believe it or not, Holmfirth now has its own vineyard.

(117) Kathy Staff once said in an interview that she thought Nora Batty has some affection for Compo but was too reserved and stubborn to ever admit this or tell him.

(118) Brian Murphy as Alvin Smedley made his first appearance in the 2003 episode The Lair of the Cat Creature.

(119) Gordon Wharmby was a decorator before he became an actor quite late in life. He appeared in acclaimed televisions productions like Edge of Darkness and A Very British Coup. Gordon died of cancer in 2002 only a few days before he was due to begin filming on Summer Wine again. Gordon Wharmby was only 68 when he died. It was a great loss to the show because Wesley Pegden had become a very familiar and likable character.

(120) Norman Wisdom made his first guest appearance in Summer Wine in the 1995 episode The Man Who Nearly Knew Pavarotti. He would appear in seven episodes in all.

(121) Colin Bennett appears in the 1999 episode Will Barry Go Septic Despite Listening to Classical Music? Colin Bennett was a familar face to early 1980s kids as Mr Bennett in the children's art show Take Hart.

(122) The formula of the 'main trio' in Summer Wine was that Cleggy and Compo are paired with someone who assumes the role of leader. Blamire, with his military bearing, assumed this role early on - though Clegg was somewhat more assertive in those early shows. Foggy naturally thought of himself as a born leader and took it upon himself to take charge of Cleggy and Compo. Foggy, though he'd be the last to admit it, was a hopeless leader though and his best laid plans were guaranteed to go wrong. Truly, as befitting a former police officer of some standing, proved to be a more competent leader than Foggy. In fact, in contrast to Foggy, a lot of Truly's plans actually worked!

(123) In the Summer Wine pilot, Wally Batty (who was unseen) was named Harold.

(124) It's a shame really that, for whatever reason, Jane Freeman as Ivy doesn't appear in the final Last of the Summer Wine episode.

(125) Last of the Summer Wine holds the Guinness World Record for the longest-running sitcom in the world.

(126) Holmfirth was not an easy location to shoot a television show because it had narrow streets.

(127) One of the obvious charms of Last of the Summer Wine is that, set in picturesque Yorkshire countryside, the show transports viewers into a simpler and more idyllic world, away from the pressures and complexities of modern life. Many of us have found comfort watching Summer Wine during difficult times in our lives.

(128) One thing which is slightly disappointing about the episodes which deal with Compo's death is that there is no appearance by Foggy or even a mention of Foggy. Brian Wilde said he declined an invitation to appear in these episodes because he didn't want the return of Foggy to distract from the show paying tribute to Compo and Bill Owen. However, it would have been a nice touch if we at least saw that Foggy had sent a wreath for Compo or a letter to Cleggy. For some reason though, Foggy is not mentioned at all.

(129) The final Summer Wine episode, How Not to Cry at Weddings, had an audience of 5.71m in Britain when it went out. Those are very decent viewing figures by today's standards.

(130) Roy Clarke said that Cleggy was the character in the show that was based the most on himself. This is probably a somewhat unsurprising fact because you wouldn't expect Roy Clarke to be like Compo or Howard or many of the other Summer Wine characters in real life!

(131) Before she died, Jean Alexander said that Auntie Wainwright was her favourite role out of all the parts she had played in her career.

(132) The veteran actress Barbara Young joined Summer Wine in 2008 as Nora Batty's sister Stella. Barbara was brought in to replace Kathy Staff. Stella was looking after Nora's house in the show and became a member of the ladies 'coffee morning'. Barbara Young also played Florrie - the wife of Barry's cousin.

(133) The comedian (and actor) Bobby Ball made three appearances in Summer Wine from 2005 to 2008 as Lenny - The Swan Man of Ilkley. Bobby's comedy partner Tommy Cannon also joined him in the show.

(134) It is impossible to say when Last of the Summer Wine 'jumped the shark' (as they say) or if it ever jumped the shark at all because this is purely subjective and down to one's personal opinion. Many people enjoyed the show in all its various eras. It would be fair to say though that some fans felt it was never quite the same when Foggy left for the last time and the show was plainly never the same without Compo when Bill Owen sadly passed away. In fact, some fans think that the touching episodes which dealt with Compo's funeral would have made a fitting swansong. What clearly didn't help either later on was the unavoidable fact that Peter Sallis was getting old and had trouble with his eyesight. The show couldn't get insurance for Peter to do outdoor scenes anymore so Cleggy became a supporting character who made cameos from his armchair - usually with Truly. Summer Wine was just not the same with Cleggy as a mere supporting character because he was always the heart of the show - the everyman who wittily observed everything and served as our window into this world.

(135) The 2000 Millennium Special episode Last Post and Pigeon, in which Compo travels (with Clegg and Truly) to France to visit World War 2 graves, was especially poignant when it first aired because Bill Owen had recently died. Bill had filmed this special and three episodes of series 21 before he died. One can plainly see that Bill is not very well in these episodes as Compo seems gaunt and frail.

(136) Julie T. Wallace, who played Mrs (Lolly Minerva) Avery, shot to fame in the BBC miniseries The Life and Loves of a She-Devil. Julie was in a Bond film too. She played Rosika Miklos in The Living Daylights - which marked the debut of Timothy Dalton as 007.

(137) Brian Glover made a guest appearance in the Summer Wine episode titled Keeping Britain Tidy. Brian played Oggie Buttercluff.

(138) Louis Emerick played PC Walsh in Last of the Summer Wine in 1988-1989 and later returned in 2004 after the death of Tony Capstick (who had previously been the sidekick to Ken Kitson as PC Cooper). Louis Emerick stayed until the end of the series. He has done many things but is best known for his role as Mick Johnson in Brookside - the famous Liverpudlian soap opera on Channel 4. Louis Emerick was in 223 episodes of Brookside.

(139) Billy Hardcastle is always complaining about his wife and sister in the show but we never actually meet them. This 'unseen character' device means we have to imagine them for ourselves.

(140) We see a shot of the grave of Clegg's wife Edith in the pilot Of Funerals and Fish.

(141) Cleggy is a key character in Summer Wine because he 'grounds' the classic main trio and is the glue that connects them. Clegg is the more realistic everyman in the middle of Compo's laid-back clowning and Foggy's pomposity and hare-brained schemes. If Clegg wasn't there as the link between them it is hard to believe that Compo and Foggy would willingly knock around with one another all the time.

(142) According to her IMDB page, Helen Turaya doesn't have any acting credits since playing Babs in Summer Wine in 2000.

(143) Bill Owen was made an honorary Yorkshireman for his part as Compo.

(144) Brian Wilde's son said in an interview that The Loxley Lozenge was a favourite episode of Brian. This is the episode were Foggy mistakes a vintage car for a cough sweet!

(145) Holmfirth is not mentioned in Last of the Summer Wine but you can see it on signposts occasionally.

(146) Marsden, Meltham, Slaithwaite and Hepworth were among the locations used in Summer Wine.

(147) John Challis, forever a British comedy legend thanks to his role as Boycie in Only Fools and Horses, appeared in the 2008 Summer Wine episode Is Jeremy Quite Safe? John Challis played a retired jewel thief hired by Auntie Wainwright to break into a safe!

(149) Mike Grady is from the West Country in real life so he was another Summer Wine cast member who had to put on a Yorkshire accent.

(150) Number 28 Huddersfield Road, the terrace house used as Nora Batty's home, was later turned into a guest cottage where Summer Wine fans could stay.

(151) Burt Kwouk as Entwistle made his first appearance in the show in the 2002 Christmas special A Musical Passing for a Miserable Muscroft.

(152) Last of the Summer Wine is slightly ambiguous about Foggy's actual war background. We know that his tales of being a deadly one-man army who single-handedly drove the Japanese out of Burma are clearly either a fantasy or highly embellished and exaggerated but his actual war record is never stated. The show establishes that Compo was at Dunkirk but although Foggy was in the army what he actually did in the war is never revealed. Maybe he really did see some action in Burma or perhaps he just painted signs away from the front lines.

(153) In the very early episodes of Summer Wine you could see that the weather was a bit grotty and wet at times. In later series they tended to avoid this by shooting on sunny days. There were episodes where it looked a bit windy and nippy but they never put the actors out in a gale force wind in the later series!

(154) In the final series of Summer Wine they actually used green screen special effects to depict Cleggy and Truly out of the house in a few scenes.

(155) Howard and Pearl's second name is Sibshaw. This is only mentioned in the show in the final series. It was mentioned earlier in a Summer Wine novel though.

(156) Danny O'Dea as Eli made his first appearance in the 1987 episode Jaws.

(157) Mike Grady said that, even when he was playing Barry in Summer Wine, he rarely got recognised in real life because, unlike Barry, he never wears a suit or tie!

(158) Summer Wine cast members who are still around get residual cheques for the repeats of the show. Last of the Summer Wine is on constant rotation on the Drama channel and long may that continue!

(159) Russ Abbot as Hobo made his first appearance in the 2008 New Year special I Was A Hitman For Primrose Dairies.

(160) Russ Abbot and June Whitfield were in another sitcom together a few years after Summer Wine ended. Russ and June were in a BBC One show called Boomers. It ran to two series and thirteen episodes before ending in 2016.

(161) Mike Grady said in an interview, many years after the show ended, that Peter Sallis was quite reclusive and self-contained as a person but would make you laugh with his dry wit. Mike said that Seymour actor Michael Aldridge was a very happy and kind person who kept everyone's spirits up and sorted out any problems the cast had.

(162) Juliette Kaplan did a one-woman stage show about Pearl, written by Roy Clarke.

(163) There were two main directors associated with Summer Wine. Sydney Lotterby and then Alan J W Bell. Alan is credited with bringing a more filmic quality to the show. He loved to get those lovely rural shots in there.

(164) Roy Clarke said he would have happily written a script for a Last of the Summer Wine feature film but no one ever asked him to.

(165) According to newspaper articles in 2023, Holmfirth is becoming quite trendy now with coffee shops, bars, and more young people. Locals seem to find this a mixed blessing.

(166) We rarely see any characters in Summer Wine watching television. Cleggy is always reading the newspaper when he's at home and there is little evidence that Cleggy even owns a television in the later series. We know that Compo owns a television though because he sometimes mentions the fact that the repo men have come to take his telly away!

(167) The episode I Was A Hitman For Primrose Dairies is dedicated to Kathy Staff. Kathy sadly died a few weeks before this episode was broadcast.

(168) A few years after Summer Wine ended, Roy Clarke teamed up with David Jason and did a sequel to his classic sitcom Open All Hours - the new show titled Still Open All Hours. Still Open All Hours, despite mixed reviews, ran to 41 episodes and six series. What is interesting about Still Open All Hours is that some dubbed it a crafty stealth continuation of Summer Wine with its large ensemble cast and gossipy women tropes! Still Open All Hours and the last few seasons of Summer Wine have some tonal and situational similarities - although that's probably to be expected given that they were written by the same person.

(169) It is said that Brian Wilde and Bill Owen didn't get on terribly well behind the scenes on Summer Wine. Their chemistry onscreen was always wonderful though.

(170) Shirley Anne Field made a guest appearance in the 2008 episode Eva's Back in Town. Shirley was in classic films like Saturday Night and Sunday Morning and Alfie. Trivia - Shirley turned down the part of Jill Masterton in the Bond film Goldfinger. This was the character who meets her end via gold paint.

(171) Jane Freeman and Peter Sallis were the only Summer Wine actors who were in all the series from beginning to end.

(172) The 2008 episode Enter The Finger was dedicated to Brian Wilde as he had died earlier that year.

(173) The Loxley Lozenge was brought forward and used as a Christmas special. This caused some continuity issues because it features Crusher and yet in the later episode Keeping Britain Tidy, we and the characters are introduced to Crusher as if we've never seen him before. DVD and television repeats amended this continuity confusion with some edits.

(174) We (the viewers) only meet Howard, Pearl, and Marina for the first time in Catching Digby's Donkey but the other characters in the show act as if they've known them for years.

(175) Stuart Fell was the main stuntman who acted as a double for Bill Owen in the heyday of the show. Stuart certainly earned his money given how many eccentric stunts Compo got involved in!

(176) Joe Gladwin played the forlorn Wally Batty, husband of Nora, in 45 episodes of Summer Wine from 1975 to 1987. It's

safe to say that (not that it was ever likely to happen) it probably wouldn't have bothered Wally in the slightest if Nora had run off with Compo! Nora definitely wore the trousers in the Batty household. Joe was a familiar face to television viewers long before Summer Wine. He played Fred Jackson in Coronation Street in the 1960s and appeared in 45 episodes of the sitcom Nearest and Dearest. Joe also appeared in some films too - like Charlie Bubbles and Yanks. Joe had Rhotacism (a difficulty producing rhotic consonants sounds) and this, combined with his thick Lancastrian accent, gave him a wonderfully distinctive voice. He featured in a lovely advert for Hovis bread during his time on Summer Wine.

(177) The real location for the (later) homes of Cleggy and Howard was Hill Street, Jackson Bridge, Holmfirth. Different homes were used earlier in the show but Cleggy and Howard were still neighbours. It could be the case that Howard followed Cleggy around!

(178) Michael Bates served with the Gurkhas in World War 2 and fought in Burma against the Japanese.

(179) Brian Murphy was obviously no stranger to comedy before appearing as Alvin in Summer Wine. He made a memorable double act with Yootha Joyce in the sitcom George & Mildred.

George & Mildred was a spin-off from Man About the House - which Brian was also obviously in. Brian said that when he joined Summer Wine he enjoyed the fact that Alvin was nothing like the George Roper character he had played in George & Mildred and Man About the House. Brian said that Summer Wine was a pleasure to do because he already knew most of the cast.

(180) Burt Kwouk was born in Manchester but was raised in Shanghai until his late teens. He then returned to England and enjoyed a very successful acting career.

(181) Eli last appeared in the episode A Brief Excursion in the Fast Lane. Poor health prevented Danny O'Dea from making any more appearances.

(182) It All Began With an Old Volvo Headlamp was the last show featuring Wesley Pegden. Gordon Wharmby passed away a few months after this episode was transmitted.

(183) The Miraculous Curing of Old Goff Helliwell featured a guest appearance by Henry McGee as Goff Helliwell - a man who has decided what day he plans to die. Henry McGee did many things but was best known for his long association with Benny Hill.

(184) Cleggy's front door is quite unusual in Summer Wine because his letterbox moves around and often seems to be at the bottom! It is plainly the case that different doors were used during the filming.

(185) Blamire was formerly a clerk with the local Water Board.

(186) There are a smattering of episodes where Norman Clegg drives a car. Cleggy plainly hates driving and is terrified behind the wheel. It's a miracle he even has a licence!

(187) First of the Summer Wine features a character named Sherbet (played by Paul Oldham) who is a friend of Clegg and Compo. Sherbert is never mentioned in Last of the Summer Wine and he never turned up in that show. The obvious implication, which makes First of the Summer Wine quite poignant, is that Sherbert was killed in the war.

(188) It is probably fair to say that Blamire had the least tolerance for Compo out of all the 'main trio' characters throughout the show. Compo did miss Blamire though when

Blamire left so Compo clearly never took their arguments and bickering as anything other than friends ribbing one another.

(189) Summer Wine initially featured Mr Wainwright (Blake Butler) and Mrs Partridge (Rosemary Martin) as the librarians. Mr Wainwright was a rather lecherous character who was always engaged in a secret (or so he thought) affair with his co-worker. Mr Wainwright returned in 1976 - this time with designs on fellow librarian Miss Moody (Kate Brown). The library was eventually written out of the show as a location - although it did obviously return many years later with Lucinda Davenport. It appears that Roy Clarke felt the librarian characters had run their course by 1976 and so phased them out of the show. Mr Wainwright rather anticipates the later character of Howard in that he is engaged in what he thinks is a secret affair but in reality it isn't secret at all.

(190) In 1975 the librarians were Miss Probert (June Watson) and Miss Jones (Janet Davies). Miss Probert was a bossy type who railed against men while Miss Jones was more timid.
Janet Davies was best known for playing Mrs Pike in Dad's Army.

(191) When he died, we learn that Compo left his ferrets to Reggie Unsworth. The characters presume Reggie is a man but it turns out to be a woman - Compo's 'Thursday Woman' to be precise. Reggie was played by Liz Fraser. Liz had an acting CV the size of a telephone directory. She was in literally everything. Hancock's Half Hour, Carry On films, The Smallest Show on Earth, Dunkirk, Jason King, Rumpole of the Bailey, Minder, Confessions films, The Avengers, and so on. Liz's last role was in an episode of Midsomer Murders in 2018.

(192) The librarian Miss Moody was the first character in Summer Wine to suffer the horror of being shown the inside of Compo's matchbox.

(193) Maggie Ollerenshaw played Ethel in two Summer Wine episodes and also made an earlier third appearance (though her character was not credited with a name). Maggie also played Norman Clegg's mother in First of the Summer Wine. Maggie is clearly a favourite of Roy Clarke because she appeared in both versions of Open All Hours - the original and the later sequel.

(194) Brian Murphy said that when the main trio was Alvin, Truly, and Clegg, he had to do all the stunts and fall in the water because, despite being in his seventies, he was considered a mere 'youngster' compared to Frank Thornton and Peter Sallis!

(195) Kathy Staff briefly left Summer Wine in 2001 to join the revival of Crossroads as her Doris Luke character.

(196) Compo was married after the war but his wife ran off with a Polish man.

(197) Frank Thornton was actually in more episodes of Summer Wine than his 'third man' predecessors. Frank was in 135 episodes. Brian Wilde as Foggy was in 116. Michael Aldridge as Seymour was in 31 episodes and Michael Bates as Blamire was only in 13.

(198) Tom Owen appeared in 93 episodes of Summer Wine in all. His first appearance was way back in 1991 as a bank customer.

(199) The librarian Mr Wainwright is no relation to Auntie Wainwright. It seems that Roy Clarke just liked the name Wainwright.

(200) Russ Abbot was only in 17 episodes of Summer Wine as Hobo. Though no one knew it at the time, the show was already nearing the end when Russ came in.

(201) Jim Bowen made a guest appearance in the Christmas special Crums. He actually appeared in three Summer Wine episodes in all. Jim Bowen was famously the host of the cult Sunday afternoon darts themed quiz show Bullseye.

(202) Marina works on the check-out at the local supermarket. It seems to be the Co-op in some episodes but later on they seemed to avoid naming a specific supermarket.

(203) Though they played husband and wife in Last of the Summer Wine, Thora Hird was 22 years older than Gordon Wharmby in real life.

(204) Gordon Wharmby only had a couple of acting credits when he was cast as Wesley in Summer Wine. Gordon said it was quite overwhelming at first to be playing scenes with the great Thora Hird - who had been acting since 1942.

(205) 'Electrical' Entwistle's real name is Mcintyre.

(206) Entwistle drives around in a pick-up truck. This was presumably done to make him something of a replacement for Wesley.

(207) Although the women in the show have a patent distaste for Marina (mainly due to Marina carrying on with the married Howard), Marina does strike up a friendship with Miss Davenport. Glenda Wilkinson is also shown to be more kind and sympathetic to Marina than the other woman.

(208) Barry Wilkinson is often in search of a hobby to make his life more interesting. He develops a fondness for golf in the end - though he often ends up annoying the club captain.

(209) Robert Fyfe appeared in three more episodes than Juliette Kaplan. So there were a few episodes where we saw Howard but not Pearl.

(210) Compo's 'costume' in Summer Wine was a tattered suit jacket, a knitted pullover with holes, a woolen hat, and some threadbare trousers with a piece of string as a belt. There was too a shirt underneath the pullover. Suffice to say, Compo is not someone who does much clothes shopping! The final piece of the outfit was of course a pair of wellies.

(211) The 1950s Phoenix bicycle used by Marina in the show sold at an auction for £500 in 2014.

(212) Bill Owen was buried at St John's Church in Holmfirth. Bill chose this spot himself while shooting Summer Wine. Peter Sallis requested that he be buried next to his old friend so when he died eighteen years later he was laid to rest in the plot next to Bill.

(213) Although he was quite a shy man who often avoided interviews, Bill Owen became very well known to the local community in Holmfirth during the production of Last of the Summer Wine. He made many new friends in the area and was very well liked.

(214) The 1983 episode The Waist Land was one of my favourites watching Summer Wine as a kid - although some seem to find this episode a trifle too silly (with the broad performances by the guest actors and the disguises at the end). In this episode, Foggy comes up with a plan to sell junk food at inflated prices to the starved inhabitants of a local health farm in the countryside. What I love about this episode is that, for a fleeting moment, a moneymaking scheme of Foggy actually works! Of course, it all goes wrong in the end though.

(215) During his time on Summer Wine, Bill Owen appeared in, among other things, the prestigious miniseries Brideshead Revisited.

(216) Ron Backhouse appeared in ten episodes of Summer Wine from 1995 to 2001. Ron was the landlord of The White Horse pub in the show - a role he also played in real life!

(217) The wonderful Geoffrey Bayldon was the guest star in the 1995 episode Adopted by a Stray. Bayldon plays Broadbent, a man who seeks wisdom in the wilderness. This episode has an especially memorable line by Cleggy - "You get up in the morning, and you never think that before the day is out, you're going to own a Mrs Broadbent!"

(218) The character of Pearl was slightly more naive when first introduced to the show. Pearl quickly became shrewd and cunning though and always one step ahead of Howard and his various schemes to escape the house to spend time with Marina.

(219) Roy Clarke chose the title of the show. He said that the characters, in terms of their lives, were in the last days of summer before autumn.

(220) The show was going to be called The Last of the Summer Wine but the first bit got chopped off in the end.

(221) It is said that the late Queen Mother was a big fan of Last of the Summer Wine.

(222) In the early 1980s, a daily comic strip based on Last of the Summer Wine was drawn by Roger Mahoney and appeared in the Daily Star.

(223) In the 1982 Christmas special All Mod Conned, Foggy decides the trio will have a relaxing break in a remote caravan. As ever though Foggy's plan turns out to be a complete disaster. The location used for the caravan was Spurn Point. Spurn is a narrow sand tidal island located off the tip of the coast of the East Riding of Yorkshire.

(224) Despite her fame, Jean Alexander lived in a modest semi-detached house in Southport, didn't own a DVD player or computer or car, had an old cathode ray telly, and did all her own shopping. She said she never married because she was perfectly happy with her own company and enjoyed being alone when she went home. After she left Coronation Street, Jean said she turned down many acting jobs but she couldn't resist playing Auntie Wainwright in Summer Wine because it was the most 'fun' part she'd ever done.

(225) Eric Sykes was a guest star in the 2007 episode The Second Stag Night of Doggy Wilkinson. Eric played Doggy, an old man with a bad memory who is about to get married. This was the last thing Eric did for the BBC.

(226) Lois Laurel, the daughter of the great Stan Laurel, has a cameo as the 'hat woman' (who has the same hat as Nora) in the 1995 episode Bicycle Bonanza. A burst of the Laurel & Hardy theme can be heard when Lois makes her exit.

(227) One difference between Wally Batty and Howard is that although they were both virtual prisoners to a stern wife, Wally would often get off a few barbs at Nora in their confrontations. Howard, by contrast, wouldn't dare to do this with Pearl!

(228) There was some fan anger at the BBC when Summer Wine got the axe. Some fans felt the BBC came off as insincere in their tributes to the show given that they'd been trying to get rid of it for years. It might have helped if Summer Wine had been allowed to bow out with a nice Christmas special - rather than just a fairly standard series.

(229) The character of Truly was something of a departure for the 'third man' formula in that Cyril Blamire, Foggy, and Seymour were all a bit pompous. Truly was, once the character got settled, a lot more relaxed than his predecessors.

Truly often mentioned his police career but he didn't come across as pompous or full of himself.

(230) Jay Hunt is the person who axed Last of the Summer Wine. She was the controller of BBC One at the time. Jay Hunt was born in Australia in 1967 and later took over at Channel 4. Alan J W Bell said that Hunt 'had it in' for Summer Wine. Jay Hunt was accused of ageism when Countryfile presenter Miriam O'Reilly was sacked from the show and this complaint was upheld in court. Hunt apparently wanted a bit more of the BBC's output to be geared towards young people, which is fair enough, but what this had to do with Summer Wine and Countryfile presenters is anyone's guess. Young people are not really your primary target audience for early evenings on Sunday are they? It is older folk who tend to be watching traditional telly at that time. The previous controller of BBC One had been more sympathetic and supportive to Last of the Summer Wine and its future but this was assuredly not the case with Jay Hunt.

(231) Brian Murphy as Alvin was initially supposed to be a one-off character who only appeared in one episode.

(232) The casting of Russ Abbot in Summer Wine was obviously an attempt to try to secure a new future for the show as Russ (who was in his early 60s at the time) was pretty young by Summer Wine standards and also quite a big star thanks to his old television show and later stage work. They could conceivably have kept the show going for years by just bringing in new characters but it wouldn't have been the same once all the old favourites were gone. Long running soap operas sort of get around this by having the grown-up children of old characters become the new characters but in Last of the Summer Wine hardly any of the characters had any children!

(233) If the show had not been cancelled and was still being made today, there would be very few old familiar characters left because nearly all of them have passed away. You could still have Barry, Glenda, and Hobo as Mike Grady, Sarah Thomas, and Russ Abbot are still with us. Ken Kitson and Louis Emerick, who played the two coppers Cooper and Walsh, are also still around. Brian Murphy is still around too but he's now 91 so Alvin would be unlikely to still be in the show - unless he made cameos from an armchair as Peter Sallis and Frank Thornton used to do near the end of the show. Maybe if the show was still around today they could have had Jonathan Linsley come back as Crusher to run the cafe!

(234) Compo's mother was a rag and bone man (or woman in this case).

(235) The series nine episode Edie and the Automobile is the first time we see Edie's comical and dangerous driving skills in action - though it is no laughing matter to the poor passengers! Edie's struggles behind the wheel became a running joke in the show - though she would blame everything on Wesley tinkering with the car!

(236) Sid doesn't appear in First of the Summer Wine although there is a character named Ivy. There is no mention of Blamire in the prequel show. Herbert Truelove isn't in the prequel show for rather obvious reasons. Frank Thornton was still some years away from joining Last of the Summer Wine so Roy Clarke hadn't invented the character of Herbert Truelove yet!

(237) Holmfirth is a former mill town and was famous for the textile industry in 18th and 19th centuries. In the very early Summer Wine episodes there is a slightly 'gritty' quality to some of the backdrops and we get a sense of a place where the old industries have died. The depiction of the backdrops in Summer Wine later on is very romantic. The locations are

lovely to look at and we even envy the characters for living in such a beautiful place.

(238) Peter Sallis, Brian Wilde, and Bill Owen performed a sketch as Cleggy, Foggy and Compo at the 1984 Royal Variety Performance.

(239) In 2023, it was reported that more people in Britain watched the repeats of Last of the Summer Wine than they did the new series of Succession!

(240) Blamire and Compo have some political disagreements in the early years of the show. This was mirrored in real life as Michael Bates was a staunch Conservative and Bill Owen was a lifelong supporter of the Labour Party.

(241) Wally Batty used to work as a station porter for the LNER (London & North Eastern Railway).

(242) Sarah Thomas as Glenda was in 215 episodes of Last of the Summer Wine from 1986 right through to the end of the show. Mike Grady, as we've mentioned, had a hiatus as Barry at one point but he wasn't written out. The unseen Barry was mentioned by Glenda as if he was still around. Presumably the producer must have known there was a good chance that Mike Grady would come back in the end so they left the door open for him. Besides, you couldn't see Barry running off with another woman or divorcing Glenda!

(243) Foggy's rank in the army was Lance Corporal Signwriter.

(244) In the prequel show, Nora Batty works at a garage and is an usherette at the local cinema.

(245) Kathy Staff's costume as Nora was a pinny, curlers, and (of course) wrinkled stockings. She usually wore a cardigan too. They gave Kathy Staff padding to make Nora seem heftier and more formidable.

(246) The opening shot in the 'pilot' of Last of the Summer Wine was of Nora Batty's house.

(247) In the prequel show First of the Summer Wine, Seymour works in the menswear department of the Co-op. Seymour is a bit of a dandy in the show. He wears huge scarves and likes driving a flash car.

(248) On the appeal of Summer Wine, Jonathan Linsley said - "It was gentle and safe. It was just a really simple story about ordinary folk."

(249) Wally Batty owned a motorbike and sidecar. Even on the road there was no escape from Nora because she was in the sidecar nagging him!

(250) Bill Owen and Joe Gladwin both appeared together in the 1982 Tales from the Unexpected episode The Moles. This episode in the classic anthology series was about a group of old men trying to rob a bank. It also starred Harry H Corbett and Fulton Mackay so it had a terrific cast.

(251) When he was asked about the apparent continuity mistake regarding Seymour being friends with Compo and Clegg in First of the Summer Wine but not seeming to know them in the base show until Uncle of the Bride, Roy Clarke said he simply hoped that viewers wouldn't notice!

(252) Foggy used to work for the local council's highways department as a sign-painter. He was in the Territorial Army just prior to the war.

(253) Last of the Summer was a midweek show at first but was eventually moved to Sunday.

(254) In reality, the front of Compo and Nora's houses are actually the exterior (back part) of the building used for this location in the show.

(255) In the prequel show, Compo gets a job at the Co-op with his friends. They obviously have to smarten Compo up a bit.

(256) Valerie Leon was a guest star in the 2006 Summer Wine episode Who's That Merry Man with Billy, Then? Valerie was in six Carry On films. She also appeared in two Bond films - The Spy Who Loved Me with Roger Moore and Never Say Never Again with Sean Connery. Never Say Never Again was an 'unofficial' Bond film that had nothing to do with the Broccoli family and was made through Kevin McClory's Thunderball rights. Her other film parts included Revenge of the Pink Panther, The Wild Geese, and The Italian Job. Valerie had a long CV in television too.

(257) Seymour, when he joined the show, was a retired headmaster who has now become a crackpot inventor. Seymour's inventor status was a plot device engineered to get Compo into comical situations and stunts.

(258) Most of the women in Last of the Summer Wine are rather domineering, gossipy, and bossy. Roy Clarke said that this aspect of the show is a Northern tradition in comedy and was also partly based on the strong, assertive and very organised women around him when he was young. Even characters like Nora and Pearl do have a softer side though. Pearl, for example, is kind and sensitive· to Cleggy when Compo dies.

(259) Juliette Kaplan said her own backstory for Pearl is that Pearl worked in a bank and Howard was a hapless customer who Pearl had to sort out some banking problem for. Pearl decided Howard was a man who needed some organisation in his life and looking after. However, this initial affection gradually turned into what you can only describe as enmity due to Howard being a dull husband and also carrying on with Marina.

(260) James Gilbert was the producer on the first series of Summer Wine. It was Gilbert who had the idea to have extensive location shooting in the show. This was fairly novel for a sitcom at the time because most sitcoms are very studio bound to keep costs down.

(261) When the first ever episode of Last of the Summer Wine went out, Ted Heath was the Prime Minister, President Nixon was beginning a second term, Elvis Presley was still performing concerts in Las Vegas, and the Vietnam war was still going on. The biggest grossing film of that year was The Exorcist.

(262) The early working title for the show was The Library Mob - which was obviously a reference to the main trio hanging around in the library a lot.

(263) Compo clearly has a sweet tooth because he puts a preposterous amount of sugar in his tea.

(264) The first series of Last of the Summer Wine was not a huge ratings hit but the BBC had enough faith in the show to give it a second series. This was a wise move because it eventually became one of their biggest hits.

(265) Amazingly, Roy Clarke wrote all the episodes of Summer Wine himself.

(266) In the first few decades of the show the interior scenes were shot in the studio in London.

(267) Cleggy, Compo, and Foggy rarely buy anything other than a cup of tea in Ivy's cafe - which would partly explain

why Ivy finds them irritating. Sometimes they will have a sticky bun and very occasionally they push the boat out and have some cooked food. Woe betide anyone who leaves a chip on their plate though because Ivy won't be happy!

(268) One theory as to why Last of the Summer Wine lasted so long in the end is that the BBC never had an obvious replacement for the show and that type of audience. Even when it ended it still had five million dedicated viewers.

(269) Bill Owen once said that Compo's obsession with Nora Batty was like a little boy with a crush. He saw Compo as essentially an innocent sort of character who meant no unease or harm to anyone.

(270) The man (Walter) who sells the trio a clapped out car in the 1973 episode The New Mobile Trio is played by Ronald Lacey. Lacey appeared in many movies and TV shows but is probably best known for playing the villain in Raiders of the Lost Ark.

(271) In the episode Return of the Warrior, we see that Cleggy and Compo are bored and at a loose end when Seymour leaves. Luckily for them , or unluckily as the case may be, Foggy Dewhurst then returns and is soon bossing them around as if he's never been away. It appears then, although they might grumble, Cleggy and Compo secretly like having someone around to get them involved in eccentric schemes. Life without Seymour or Foggy would certainly be a lot less stressful but it would also be far less interesting.

(272) Although he was from Yorkshire, Roy Clarke wasn't familiar with Holmfirth at all when it was first mooted as a location. Roy didn't even know where Holmfirth was.

(273) All the stuff about Hobo claiming to be a former spy was toned down somewhat in the last series of Summer Wine. Roy

Clarke and Russ Abbot were modifying and improving the character somewhat. Sadly though the show was axed before Hobo could truly find his feet as a character.

(274) Amazingly, the BBC initially disliked Ronnie Hazlehurst's legendary theme tune for Last of the Summer Wine! The BBC wanted something more upbeat and 'sitcom'. Thankfully though they didn't get their way.

(275) Roy Clarke said that Last of the Summer was never meant to be realistic or about the past. The show takes place in a rather idyllic make believe world where everyone knows each other and life is a bit slower and more whimsical than the real world.

(276) Foggy Dewhurst is a bit tight when it comes to money. He keeps his change in a little purse - which Cleggy and Compo often make light of.

(277) The character of Seymour seems to have a rather worrying enthusiasm for corporal punishment! "What do you mean, you're not allowed to hit small boys? That's what they're for!"

(278) Around the time that Last of the Summer was starting and finding its feet, Bill Owen appeared in four episodes of another classic sitcom - Whatever Happened to the Likely Lads? Bill played the father of Brigit Forsyth's Thelma. Brigit was later in 41 episodes of Roy Clarke's Still Open All Hours.

(279) Peter Sallis said that when they started work on the first series of Summer Wine, the producer James Gilbert banned Michael Bates and Bill Owen from talking about politics because the subject was provoking too many arguments between them. Peter said that he wasn't a very political or opinionated person himself so he was the neutral middle man in all of this. A bit like Clegg you might say!

(280) Long before Summer Wine, Peter Sallis worked on the stage with big names like, among others, Vivien Leigh, Laurence Olivier, and John Gielgud.

(281) The series two episode The Changing Face of Rural Blamire is a novelty because the main trio actually get a job. Well, Blamire does at least. Cleggy and Compo tag along and help out - the trio working as door to door salesmen selling 'ShinyGlow' Products. As you might expect, things do not go very well.

(282) Compo never has any money and what little he does accrue he fritters away in the betting shop. He was never that bothered by material things though anyway.

(283) In the prequel series First of the Summer Wine, Cleggy's mother is shown to be a rather nervous woman who worried a lot. This is clearly where Clegg got his neurotic qualities from.

(284) Auntie Wainwright seems to have elaborate security at her shop. She can lock people in, has an intimidating loudspeaker system, and has even been known to brandish a shotgun!

(285) Crusher was a rather simple minded chap. It's a common sitcom trope to have a character who isn't very bright.

(286) Barry Wilkinson is fond of golf but way back in the 1976 episode The Kink in Foggy's Niblick we saw Foggy playing an epic round of golf in which he frequently went preposterously out of bounds. What didn't help is that Foggy hadn't played golf since 1939 so he was a bit rusty!

(287) Despite the fact that Crusher, with his thick black hair and burly build, sort of resembles a younger version of Sid, he is from Ivy's side of the family.

(288) There is touching moment in the Compo funeral episode when Ivy looks at a photograph of Sid and smiles. It's a nice touch to have a little poignant reminder of this character and John Comer.

(289) The initial plan was for Last of the Summer Wine to be set in Rotherham. In the end though they decided that town was a little bit too urban for the show they had in mind.

(290) Some of the episode Last Post and Pigeon was shot on location in France.

(291) The enjoyable 1976 episode The Great Boarding-House Bathroom Caper is something of a novelty because the characters take a short holiday at the seaside in Scarborough. It is rare to see everyone out of their usual surroundings.

(292) A stage play based on Roy Clarke's book Last of the Summer Wine - The Moonbather has occasionally run since 2003. The synopsis for the novel goes like this - 'Seymour Utterthwaite decides to make a play for Gifford Bewmont's fiancee, Samantha Pettit. He invites her to a soiree at Clegg's house but his little party is invaded by Compo and also by the "streaker" who has been haunting the neighbourhood and turns out to be none other than ...'

(293) The 1980s Last of the Summer Wine stage show was very popular. In 1987 the title of the show was changed to Compo Plays Cupid due to the fact that Peter Sallis had dropped out and Bill Owen was the only one of the main trio left in it. Peter obviously stayed in the television show but presumably wanted a rest from doing the stage version.

(294) There was a degree of snootiness towards Last of the Summer Wine in its final years. It would sometimes top polls of shows that the viewers apparently wanted to axe. The samples in these polls were not exactly large though and most of the people who moaned about Summer Wine had never even seen much of the show anyway. Last of the Summer Wine only took up a modest half hour of the BBC's weekly output so the complaints seemed a bit bizarre. All of us have television shows we don't care for very much but we tend to simply watch something else and leave the people who enjoy them in peace.

(295) Clegg's wife Edith does not make an appearance in First of the Summer Wine. Cleggy had obviously not met Edith yet during the time the prequel show is set.

(296) Roy Clarke said that each time they had to replace a member of the main trio he feared that the show might not survive. Thankfully though the replacements, saliently Brian Wilde as Foggy, Michael Aldridge as Seymour, and Frank Thornton as Truly, turned out to be good enough to keep the show going.

(297) The birth year of Cleggy's wife Edith is somewhat obscured and vague when we see her heasdstone in the 'pilot' episode.

(298) Tom Simmonite's puppet dog is named Waldo.

(299) Tom Simmonite had a Renault van when he first arrived in the show but this seemed to disappear quite quickly. Maybe the repo man took it away!

(300) Bill Owen read the first script for Summer Wine in bed one night and thought it was fantastic. He agreed to take part soon afterwards. He obviously went to sleep first though!

(301) Roy Clarke said the trick to writing Summer Wine is that he approached the main trio not as old men but as kids who had just got a bit older.

(302) Roy Clarke said that, oddly, apart from him no one seemed to much like Last of the Summer Wine as a title for the show - not even the cast. However, no one could think of anything better so this title stayed in place.

(303) Last of the Summer Wine 'merch' has included clotted cream Last of the Summer Wine toffees.

(304) Compo meets his end when the sight of Nora Batty in her chorus girl outfit is too much for his heart. Ivy had suggested that Nora surprise Compo in this outfit as they were walking home from their charity cabaret practice. Nora feels some guilt about this but Compo did die happy because Nora attempted to revive him through mouth to mouth. Cleggy later deduces that Compo seemed to be getting his affairs in order before he died and left a letter for him. This obviously suggests that Compo was poorly and knew he was going to die so it wasn't really Nora's fault. Compo's death happens offscreen for obvious reasons.

(305) Roy Clarke said he found it a very delicate task to write the episodes which deal with Compo's death because he had to balance comedy and tragedy in a way that the show had never done before.

(306) Although the character of Cleggy feels slightly more assertive and abrasive in the early episodes, Peter Sallis said he played Clegg the same way all through the show and never noticed any change.

(307) Brian Wilde went straight into Last of the Summer Wine after completing work on the last series of Porridge. He did return to play Mr Barrowclough again though in the 1979 film version of Porridge.

(308) Louis Emerick's 'second police officer' only got a name (PC Walsh) in the 29th series.

(309) It is probably fair to say that Entwistle worked a bit better as a supporting character who popped in and out of the show than he did as part of the main trio at the end of Last of the Summer Wine. Burt Kwouk, rather like Brian Murphy, felt a bit sidelined when Russ Abbot became the 'leader' of the trio.

(310) Roy Clarke said that Compo was based on real life 'feckless but cheerful' people he had known in Yorkshire when he was younger.

(311) Brian Wilde said that the character of Foggy was appealing to him because Foggy Dewhurst was nothing like Mr Barrowclough. Mr Barrowclough was a meek ditherer whereas Foggy was a man who, however incompetent he might be, always tried to take charge of a situation.

(312) One of Foggy's great ambitions was to be hired to walk the Queen's corgis. Foggy thought this would make him short odds for an OBE - or even a knighthood!

(313) Some fans, though obviously not all, felt the Howard/Marina/Pearl antics got a bit played out in the end. Many of the plots later on would revolve around Howard and his desperate attempts to get a message to Marina or even simply slip away from Pearl and leave the house. Howard and Pearl were very popular characters though and so they understandably came to be used more and more as the show went on. One can't deny that Robert Fyfe was always wonderfully committed to his performance as the sly Howard and Juliette Kaplan is equally good as the sarcastic and formidable Pearl.

(314) Terry Wogan played a small part in the success of Last of the Summer Wine because he used to muse on radio about Nora Batty and Doris Luke in Crossroads (both played by Kathy Staff of course) being sisters!

(315) Seymour's lovely country home in Summer Wine, complete with pond, is a real house in Hepworth. It is now a private home and farm. They didn't use it much in the show - presumably because they couldn't get permission to do more shooting. The interior scenes in Seymour's house were done in the studio.

(316) Peter Sallis said he always thought of Last of the Summer Wine as a sort of sitcom version of The Wind in the Willows.

(317) The title of the 1990 episode Das Welly Boot, where Foggy decides to restore an old boat, is a pun on the 1981 German film (and also miniseries) Das Boot by Wolfgang Petersen. Das Boot is a gripping and brilliantly acted drama about life on a U-boat during World War 2.

(318) In the episode Uncle of the Bride when Foggy reverses the car into the pond, on the first take Peter Sallis went too fast and the car was totally submerged and started sinking! They had to do another take - this time with doubles rather than actors.

(319) Compo is very fond of apple tart and custard. We know this because he requests it from Nora - just prior to getting a bucket of water over his head!

(320) There is a fish and chip shop in Holmfirth named after Compo. Compo's is located at 9 Burnlee Rd, Holmfirth. The reviews of this chippy are very good and there are lovely surroundings outside to eat.

(321) Sid's Cafe in Holmfirth, which you can visit now in real life, offers a menu of sandwiches and toasted sandwiches, homemade soup, toast, and jacket potatoes. They also serve scones, teacakes, and fruitcake. It is generally traditional English cafe grub.

(322) Nora Batty is a regular at church. This is something that Kathy Staff had in common with the character.

(323) Brian Murphy's Alvin had a different sort of relationship to Nora than Compo when he became her neighbour. Alvin had no romantic interest in Nora. He simply wanted to make her laugh or smile - which is definitely not an easy task!

(324) The first ever line in Last of the Summer Wine was by Nora Batty. The line was - "They're taking his telly again."

(325) The 1990 episode Barry's Christmas was Mike Grady's last appearance until the 1996 Christmas Special Extra! Extra!

(326) In some of the older episodes such is the clutter of Compo's house that we must presume he is something of a hoarder!

(327) Barbara Young, after playing Florrie in the show, was a trifle confused when she was brought back - this time as Nora's sister Stella. Barbara had assumed she was coming back to play Florrie again. She had no idea she was playing a new character!

(328) Russ Abbot was able to do more stunts and physical stuff in Summer Wine than other cast members because he was a relative youngster compared to most of them.

(329) Roy Clarke deliberately wrote the character of Glenda Wilkinson so that as she gets older she becomes more like her mother Edie.

(330) The BBC got a great many letters of protest when they axed Last of the Summer Wine. Not that it made any difference. Their minds were made up. The BBC didn't do themselves many favours by keeping the decision to cancel Summer Wine to themselves for quite a long time before they made it public or let the cast know.

(331) Although there is a contradiction between Last of the Summer Wine and First of the Summer Wine in regard to when Cleggy and Compo met Seymour, Last of the Summer Wine later seemed to try to correct this by having Seymour appear to make references to knowing Compo at school.

(332) Sid and Ivy's cafe was more grotty and spartan at the start of the show compared to the more cosy cafe of later series.

(333) It's a bit jarring to have Peter Sallis play Norman Clegg's father in First of the Summer Wine because we have to suspend disbelief to think that Cleggy grew up to be an identical twin of his father in terms of looks but they do at least give Peter a mustache! In the prequel show we see that Cleggy's father was a man of few words who had an obsession with painting the family gate.

(334) There were 295 episodes of Last of the Summer Wine. It was a bit mean of the Beeb not to let it get up to 300!

(335) Roy Clarke apparently didn't visit the set of Last of the Summer Wine very much. He simply delivered the scripts and preferred not to interfere with the production of the show. The same was true on First of the Summer Wine. Cast members on that show said they only saw Roy once - if that.

(336) When the show came to an end, editions of Countryfile and Songs of Praise came from Holmfirth as a tribute to Last of the Summer Wine.

(337) We never see Nelly's husband Travis - although she often mentions him. Travis needs a lot of looking after by all accounts.

(338) Although he plainly IS a thin man, Nora hates it whenever anyone says Wally is thin because she prides herself on feeding her husband well.

(339) Nora worked at the cafe as a waitress for Ivy in later series. Nora and Ivy loved a good gossip about the customers.

(340) Compo slurps his tea from a saucer rather than drink it from a cup. Foggy in particular is revolted by this!

(341) Nora Batty is sometimes critical of the sponge cakes made by other women in Last of the Summer Wine. Nora clearly prides herself on making a good sponge cake.

(342) Foggy Dewhurst considers himself to be a master of camouflage.

(343) The Man Who Nearly Knew Pavarotti was the first episode of the show to use a widescreen ratio.

(344) Jonathan Linsley as Crusher Milburn was only in 20 episodes of Last of the Summer Wine. Jonathan also made an appearance in one episode of First of the Summer Wine as a character named Chunky Livesey.

(345) Alan J W Bell and Sydney Lotterby are most associated with Last of the Summer Wine when it comes to directors but they weren't the only ones who directed on the show. James Gilbert directed the first series and Bernard Thompson directed the second series. Bernard Thompson was also a director on shows like Whatever Happened to the Likely Lads? and Only Fools and Horses.

(346) Nora's range of hats in Summer Wine are rather mocked by Ivy at times.

(347) Norman Clegg is the philosopher of Last of the Summer

Wine. His amusing philosophical musings are often a highlight of episodes.

(348) Hobo lives in the same row of houses as Cleggy, Howard and Pearl.

(349) The Last Surviving Maurice Chevalier Impression has Compo, as the title implies, impersonating Maurice Chevalier in an attempt to impress Nora Batty. Maurice Chevalier (born September 12, 1888) was a French actor, singer, and entertainer. He rose to fame in the early 20th century and became one of France's most beloved performers. He appeared in several Hollywood movies, including Gigi, for which he received an Academy Award nomination. It is possible that Roy Clarke might have been inspired by the 1932 Marx Brothers film Monkey Business. A particular highlight in Monkey Business comes when the Marx Brothers, who are stowaways on a cruise ship, all pose as Maurice Chevalier singing "You Brought a New Kind of Love to Me" in an attempt to blag their way through passport control and exit the ship.

(350) The 1990 episode Das Welly Boot is the first one where Cleggy and Howard (who are always neighbours - much to the frequent dismay of Cleggy!) are in the homes they would stay in until the series ended.

(351) A number of Summer Wine cast members, notably June Whitfield, Juliette Kaplan, and Jane Freeman, were very critical of the BBC when the axe loomed over Last of the Summer Wine. June Whitfield accused the BBC of ageism and said it was full of young executives who didn't seem to understand that older people watched television too.

(352) Nora Batty has an encyclopedic knowledge of births, deaths, and marriages in the area, and the current whereabouts of literally everyone the characters in the show have ever known. Nora is like a living Wikipedia!

(353) According to a poll by the survey site YouGov, 83% of the British public have heard of Last of the Summer Wine.

(354) The survey site YouGov, through their polling on television shows, ranks Last of the Summer Wine as the 170th most popular television show of all time in Britain. The number one spot was taken by Only Fools and Horses.

(355) Roy Barraclough was the guest star in the 2005 episode Has Anyone Seen a Peruvian Wart? Roy played Corcroft - a man who considers himself to be a smooth ladykiller. Roy Barraclough was best known for his role as Alec Gilroy in Coronation Street and also his long association with Les Dawson (Roy and Les would play the gossipy ladies in a famous sketch).

(356) Only five cast members in the history of Last of the Summer Wine appeared in more episodes than Jean Fergusson. Jean (as Marina obviously) only came into the show in 1985 and she got less scenes than Howard and Pearl so her episode tally is very impressive

(357) Burt Kwouk appeared in five more episodes of Summer Wine than Brian Murphy. Burt was in 78 episodes. Burt came into the show a year earlier than Brian.

(358) James Duggan appeared in six episodes of Last of the Summer Wine from 1985 to 1990 as the pub landord. Duggan had a long CV and appeared in everything from Minder to Coronation Street.

(359) A frequent staple of the second Foggy Dewhurst era was an early scene in each episode where Foggy would suddenly start talking to some bemused stranger about snipers or the correct way to bayonet someone. Foggy would depict himself as a great hero to the people of Burma - who worshipped him like a god if Foggy is to be believed (and let's be honest, Foggy probably isn't to be believed). Foggy Dewhurst is a man who tends to see everything through a military themed prism. Take him up on a beautiful peaceful hill and he'll start talking about the ways he would defend that vantage point with a machine gun nest!

(360) Pearl's main punishment for Howard is taking away his freedom to actually go outside on his own but he is also forced to endlessly the wash the windows on the house. Pearl must have the cleanest windows in Yorkshire!

(361) We very occasionally see Compo's bedroom in the show. Mostly though, when we go in Compo's house we only see his threadbare and scruffy basement living room.

(362) A lot of the characters in Last of the Summer Wine wear flat caps. There was a time when the flat cap was traditional head gear for the humble working-class man. These days though the flat cap has been hijacked by hipsters and celebrities.

(363) The great Ron Moody was a guest star in the episode Captain Clutterbuck's Treasure. Moody played Lieutenant Commander Willoughby - a man who sells a treasure map to Foggy, Compo, and Clegg.

(364) Blaimire considers himself to be a high class sort of chap and prides himself on his tidy appearance and alleged status. It is therefore something of an affront to his dignity that he lives in lodgings and has to walk his landlady's dog.

(365) Alan J W Bell said the appeal of Last of the Summer Wine was that it offered "clean, British humour" in an increasingly cynical and tasteless television landscape.

(366) Last of the Summer Wine was sold to more than 25 countries. It has fans around the world.

(367) Peter Sallis said that there was certainly some of his own personality in Cleggy - much more so than other characters he played in his career.

(368) Stanley Lebor was a guest star in the 1999 episode The Phantom No 14 Bus. Stanley Lebor did many things but is probably best known as Howard in the sitcom Ever Decreasing Circles.

(369) Barry Wilkinson's pride and joy is his car. We often see him washing his car.

(370) Nora Batty seems to have an obsession with a clean front step. Brushing and scouring this step is an essential part of her day.

(371) Because the show did a lot of outdoor location work in Yorkshire, there were often a crowd of people watching the shooting. The locals were obviously kept far enough away not to interfere with the filming.

(372) The local council in the Holmfirth area were cooperative with the BBC when it came to Last of the Summer Wine because they felt the show would be good for the town and tourism.

(373) A common device in Roy Clarke's scripts is that the main trio will meet some eccentric character in the countryside, a real barnpot as Cleggy might say, who has some crazy mad scheme or invention. The main trio will end up helping out - leading to inevitable comic capers.

(374) Compo is usually the most cheerful and carefree of men. However he is occasionally prone to bouts of depression whenever he suspects that Nora Batty has any interest in another man (which - in reality - Nora definitely doesn't). Compo was very put out and jealous when Smiler became Nora's lodger.

(375) Wesley is always working on cars and engines in his shed so he's usually covered in grease and oil. You can't really blame Edie for putting newspapers down on the floor whenever Wesley has to come into the kitchen!

(376) Juliette Kaplan said in an interview for a Summer Wine documentary that the thing which prevents the Howard/Marina/Pearl triangle from being tawdry or tragic is the knowledge that Howard would never actually do anything with Marina even if he had the chance!

(377) Auntie Wainwright is so mean that when she makes a pot of tea she only uses one t-bag!

(378) The location used for Edie and Wesley's house in Last of the Summer Wine is Spring Lane, Holmbridge.

(379) Digley Reservoir was often used for location shooting in Last of the Summer Wine. Digley Reservoir is a lake located downstream of Bilberry Reservoir, 2 miles south west of Holmfirth.

(380) Barry Wilkinson is often seen enjoying a boiled egg for his breakfast before he departs for the building society. Glenda is always very proud of Barry's occupation. She acts as if he's some City of London hotshot executive!

(381) There are some scenes in Last of the Summer Wine where Bill Owen as Compo walks past the spot where he was later laid to rest in real life.

(382) Smiler's nickname is of course ironic because one thing

he definitely never does is smile.

(383) Although the character of Tom Simmonite seems to divide Summer Wine fans, he did work better later on when he was teamed up with Smiler and worked for Auntie Wainwright. Tom Owen seemed more relaxed in the role later on and gave a better performance than he did in his early episodes - where he seemed to be trying a bit too hard and often over-egged his part as a consequence.

(384) Late on in the show, Hobo becomes convinced that Nelly is his mother - something which irritates Nelly quite a lot.

(385) The 1993 Christmas special Welcome to Earth includes a little homage to E.T. the Extra-Terrestrial.

(386) Ronnie Hazelhurst said he was asked to speed up the Summer Wine theme tune at first to make it feel more like a sitcom tune. Thankfully it was allowed to stay as it was.

(387) George Chakiris made a guest appearance in the episode Extra! Extra! Chakiris is best known for the 1961 film West Side Story - he played Bernardo Nunez.

(388) The 1997 episode A Sidecar Named Desire is the last one that Brian Wilde ever appeared in.

(389) From series nineteen onwards, each episode had an intro (cold open) before the titles. They only used to do this occasionally in previous series.

(390) Cyril Blamire was a "supply wallah" (a storeman) in India during the war. Blamire is a bit like Foggy in that, even in civilian life, he still has a military bearing about him. It's no surprise that Blamire and Foggy were friends because these two men have a lot in common!

(391) Michael Bates was in some amazing things and had a fascinating career. Not just Frenzy, Patton, and A Clockwork Orange. He was also in The Stone Tape. The Stone Tape is a spooky 1972 BBC television play directed by Peter Sasdy and written by Nigel Kneale of Quatermass fame. Like Jonathan Miller's BBC MR James adaption Whistle And I'll Come To You, The Stone Tape was first shown at Christmas and is both fondly remembered and generally regarded to be one of the more scary things transmitted on British television over the years. In 1972, Bates was also memorable in an episode of Public Eye called Horse and Carriage. Public Eye was a brilliant private detective show with Alfred Burke. Peter Sallis was also in an episode of Public Eye. Bates also won great acclaim for Inspector Truscott in the West End production of Loot by Joe Orton in 1966.

(392) The track and field hero Kriss Akabusi made a guest appearance as a milkman in the 1997 episode There Goes the Groom.

(393) The train station used in the episode From Audrey Nash to the Widow Dilhooley is Huddersfield. This is the episode where Truly learns that an old flame is coming to town.

(394) Brian Wilde had an uncredited role as a policeman in the Bond film You Only Live Twice.

(395) Billy Hardcastle believes he is a direct descendant of Robin Hood. Billy seems to have a theory that Robin Hood was from Yorkshire.

(396) Ken Kitson as PC Cooper sported a rather luxurious mustache in some of the earlier episodes.

(397) What makes the episode Elegy For Fallen Wellies especially touching is that when Cleggy talks about Compo he is clearly expressing too the thoughts of Peter Sallis on missing his friend Bill Owen.

(398) Although the snootier retrospectives of Summer Wine sometimes suggest the show got silly when the comical stunts became a staple, they did actually make the show more popular - especially with kids. And there were plenty of classic episodes too beyond the Blamire years so it isn't as if there was any decline in quality when it came to the acting and Roy Clarke's wonderful dialogue. It is probably fair to say that the show got a bit tired at times near the very end of its long run (and one unavoidably missed some of the old favourites who had passed away or were now reduced to brief cameos) but it was still always watchable and enjoyable right to the end.

(399) In 2023, dancers Deborah Sanderson and Vince Virr performed an aerial routine outside the Holmfirth Picturedrome dressed as Nora Batty and Compo to promote the Holmfirth Arts Festival.

(400) The Loxley Lozenge features the chassis of a vintage car Wesley has found. The name of the car (Loxley Lozenge) is fictional and was invented purely for the episode.

(401) Wesley Pegdens jeep is a Land Rover.

(402) Cleggy's fear of driving comes from the fact that when he was married he had a temperamental car which would sometimes reverse instead of accelerating. This turned him into a nervous driver who was uncomfortable behind the wheel.

(403) Edie always drove a Triumph Herald car in Last of the Summer Wine.

(404) Hobo's real name is Luther Hobdyke.

(405) Hobo is a retired milkman. Alvin and Entwistle seem to suggest that Hobo wasn't a very good milkman!

(406) One of the strengths of the classic episode Full Steam Behind is that the focus is entirely on Cleggy, Compo, and Foggy. In later years the show would become more of a 'collective' with a larger group of characters.

(407) Bill Owen, although he insisted on carrying on and was determined to complete his scenes, was 85 and in poor health during his last days on Last of the Summer Wine. Mike Grady said an interview many years later that Bill would shoot a scene and then slump in his chair exhausted. Mike said that he will always remember Bill Owen as a very brave man who was a true professional - right to the end.

(408) On the last batch of episodes that Bill Owen was involved in they didn't manage to shoot all the interior scenes before Bill fell ill and sadly passed away. They had to use some older footage of Bill and body doubles to complete these scenes.

(409) You can now buy a DVD set which includes every series of Last of the Summer Wine. It would take you a long time to get through that!

(410) Peter Sallis wore some of his real old clothes as Cleggy when Last of the Summer Wine first started.

(411) Entwistle is a jack of all trades. Not only is he an electrician but he's also a fortune teller and washing machine salesman!

(412) Kenneth Cope appeared in two episodes of Summer Wine - The Love Mobile and All That Glitters Is Not Elvis. Kenneth Cope was in many things but is probably best known for his role as Marty in the cult supernatural detective show

Randall and Hopkirk (Deceased).

(413) Although the world the characters inhabit in Last of the Summer Wine often seems anachronistic or old-fashioned, we do see Barry Wilkinson using a laptop computer quite a lot.

(414) Roy Clarke said that while Norman Clegg was written with Peter Sallis in mind he wasn't involved in the casting of Compo and Blamire and made no suggestions as to what actors might play these characters. It obviously turned out perfect in the end though because they got Bill Owen and Michael Bates.

(415) Roy Clarke said that, although it was still summer when they shot the first episode of Last of the Summer Wine, it was actually quite nippy up on the moors with a wind coming in.

(416) Tony Melody, who dubbed John Comer's lines in Getting Sam Home due to John's illness, later played a pub landlord in the 2003 episode The Second Husband and the Showgirls. This is the episode where the husband of Truly's former wife (the former Mrs Truelove - as Truly would say) turns up.

(417) In the first script notes for what became the Last of the Summer Wine pilot, Nora Batty is described as a 'fat, dreadful looking woman'.

(418) We never actually get a first name for Auntie Wainwright in the show.

(419) Repeats of Last of the Summer Wine were reported to have got a huge ratings boost during the pandemic lockdowns. It was the perfect show to use as a means to escape from the world and its troubles.

(420) Bill Owen was nearly 60 when he got the part of Compo. Bill's career was somewhat on the wane at the time. This probably explains why Bill loved Compo and Summer Wine so much. It gave him a whole new career later in life.

(421) In the episode Magic And The Morris Minor, Auntie Wainwright is told by her doctor that it isn't good to constantly scrimp and save and that she should spend some money for a change and enjoy herself. To this end, Auntie Wainwright goes to Ivy's cafe and orders the most expensive cream cake on the menu. This is a cream slice which costs 75p. However, Auntie Wainwright - as ever - then has an attack of tightness. She takes the cake back to the shop and sells it to Smiler for a pound!

(422) In the episode Under the Rug, Auntie Wainwright makes another attempt to spend some money at Ivy's cafe but after learning of the prices for breakfast she simply orders half a cup of tea!

(423) Kathy Staff's original audition for Nora Batty was a last minute job in which she was nearly late. Fate though had obviously decided that Kathy would play this part. You couldn't imagine anyone else as Nora.

(424) Peter Sallis, Jean Alexander, and Robert Fyfe were all in their 90s when they died. While it is sad they are no longer around they certainly had a good innings and provided us with many hours of happy entertainment.

(425) Jane Freeman said of the character of cafe owner Ivy - "I'm like one of those seaside-postcard battleaxes."

(426) When the show became more of an ensemble there were usually a checklist of staple scenes. A visit to the cafe, ladies coffee session, a visit to Wesley's shed, Barry and Glenda having breakfast, the captive Howard trying to work out how to get a message to Marina, Compo bantering with Nora outside her house, and so on.

(427) Barry and Glenda occasionally talk about the prospect of having children but they never actually had any kids in the show. Mike Grady and Sarah Thomas were both knocking on a bit in the later years of the show so in the end they couldn't really depict them as a young couple thinking about having children in the future anymore.

(428) It was generally recorded that Keith Clifford (as Billy) left Summer Wine so he could take other acting jobs but it has been reported too that Keith Clifford had a bad back and left the show for health reasons. Keith was the daft younger one in the Clegg/Truly/Billy trio so the lion's share of any slapstick or stunt comedy fell on him.

(429) Auntie Wainwright is said in the show to own most of Stackpole Street. She clearly has more wealth and money than her clothes and penny pinching would suggest but she just can't help being mean and miserly.

(430) Smiler has a white convertible 1972 Chevrolet Impala. Auntie Wainwright occasionally uses this car for promotional purposes.

(431) Colin Farrell (not THAT Colin Farrell obviously) made two appearances in Last of the Summer Wine as Clegg's cousin Aubrey. Aubrey was a right pain in the you know what. He was very bossy and controlling and made Cleggy a virtual prisoner in his own house. Aubrey wouldn't even let Cleggy go out to play with his friends!

(432) Cleggy's last house in Summer Wine has a rather strange door at times. The door sometimes looks like it belongs in a stable!

(433) Philip Jackson appeared in three 1976 episodes as Compo's nephew Gordon Simmonite. Gordon joined the characters when they went to Scarborough. Thereafter,

Gordon never appeared in the show again. It might be a case that Philip Jackson (who was a busy actor in many things) was unavailable but it seems more likely that Roy Clarke decided to remove the characters related to Compo. The general concept behind Last of the Summer Wine's classic main trio is that they don't have any responsibilities or connections (like wives, children, family etc) so knock around together to pass the time and have some company. This concept doesn't work as well if Compo has numerous relatives constantly popping in and out of the show.

(434) There was no explanation in the show for why the character of Babs Avery disappeared. It appears that Babs didn't really work in the show and was just quietly dropped.

(435) Gordon Simmonite married Josie (played by Liz Goulding) in the show. Josie Simmonite, like Gordon, is another character that was dropped from the show quite sharpish and didn't become a regular.

(436) Seymour was married to Miriam Utterthwaite. Miriam left Seymour because his inventions drove her mad! Miriam is mentioned in the show more than once but we never actually see her.

(437) Entwistle is married but we never see his wife.

(438) It is probably fair to say that the early episodes with Blamire had less plot and simpler scenarios than the later episodes in decades to come. The later episodes had more characters and the situations that the main trio got into with Foggy were more elaborate and outlandish than the ones with Blamire.

(439) In the early episode The New Mobile Trio, Cleggy shoves a kid off a Road Safety Exhibition Driving Simulator so he can have a go himself. You can't imagine the Clegg of later

series doing something like this!

(440) Blamire, Cleggy, and Compo, mirror - intentionally one would imagine - the class system. Blamire is a Tory who had a white-collar job, Compo is an unemployed scruff who hates authority, and Clegg is the everyman in the middle.

(441) In the early episodes of Summer Wine there is a noticeable difference between the film stock quality of the exterior scenes and interior scenes.

(442) First of the Summer Wine was slightly more realistic and less broad in tone than Last of the Summer Wine. First of the Summer Wine sometimes feels more like a gentle comic drama than a sitcom. This is especially the case with the pilot.

(443) Compo's wife ran away and left him in 1947. Compo has no idea what happened to his wife or whether she is still alive.

(444) Eli Woods and James Casey made five appearances in Last of the Summer Wine together as drunks. Woods and Casey were comedians and also cousins. Their last appearance was in 2006.

(445) Last of the Summer Wine occasionally did some shooting near the River Calder.

(446) There was a gap of two years between Wesley Pegden's first appearance and his second appearance.

(447) In the episode The Arts of Concealment, Foggy causes a group of cyclists to crash when he attempts to demonstrate camouflage techniques. The cyclists used were from the Yorkshire Terrier Cycle Collective.

(448) Last of the Summer Wine appealed to different generations because many of us can remember watching it as

both children and then much later adults. Because the show went out on a Sunday I'm sure many of us associate it with that dreaded feeling of knowing there is school tomorrow!

(449) Roy Clarke said that Peter Sallis delivered Clegg's lines brilliantly and never asked for anything in a script to be changed.

(450) The comedy in the character of Foggy Dewhurst comes from his unshakable but misplaced self-belief. Foggy doesn't realise that the main reason Cleggy and Compo go along with his barmy schemes is that it amuses them to anticipate the moment when it will eventually go wrong!

(451) Roy Clarke said that the main reason he got rid of the library and library characters fairly early in the show is that he was struggling to think of new ideas or scenes for the library. In the early years of the show, Blamire, Cleggy, and Compo go to the library to read the newspapers. Because they are struggling to find ways to pass the time the library is somewhere they gravitate towards because you don't have to pay to get in!

(452) Derek Etchells made two appearances in the early seasons of Last of the Summer Wine as the 'repo man' Eric. We see Eric repossessing things from Compo's house. Compo is so used to the repo men he leaves the door unlocked for them!

(453) Hobo, who became the 'leader' of the last main trio in the show, doesn't really get an introduction episode in the way that Foggy, Seymour, and Truly did. Hobo is just sort of suddenly there in the show one day.

(454) Compo has a number of insults for Foggy. Perhaps his favourite though is to call Foggy a 'great long dollop'!

(455) The ladies coffee morning scenes would often end with

the women drinking their coffee/tea in synchronised fashion.

(456) In the episode Return of the Warrior, Nora Batty and Ivy both show a bit of rare affection and kindness to Foggy when they welcome him home.

(457) In the prequel show First of the Summer Wine, the building which would later become Sid's Cafe is a fish and chip shop. The name of the shop is Hygenic Fisheries.

(458) Jean Fergusson said the scenes in the show where Howard and Marina end up in water were no picnic because it was usually freezing and the water in some of the canals they filmed in was rather on the dirty side!

(459) Peter Sallis and Frank Thornton were born in the same year only a few days apart.

(460) Gary Whitaker does a very credible impersonation of Joe Gladwin as Wally Batty in First of the Summer Wine. Whitaker manages to capture Joe's unique way of speaking.

(461) Compo will often say Tha' - which is Yorkshire slang for You.

(462) One of Compo's favourite words is 'chuffing'. 'Chuffin' eck' is basically a Yorkshire way of swearing without actually swearing!

(463) Roy Clarke said he was disappointed that First of the Summer Wine was axed by the BBC because he had hoped to write some episodes where you see these characters during World War 2.

(464) Foggy Dewhurst's idea of a good time is to go on a brisk route march in rough terrain!

(465) A Compo outfit worn by Bill Owen in the show in the late 1990s fetched £6,000 at an auction after Summer Wine ended.

(466) Peter Sallis said in his autobiography that Bill Owen, to get fully into character, would fill Compo's pockets with childlike things like conkers and pieces of string.

(467) It is a great credit to Brian Wilde and the writing of Roy Clarke that only a few episodes into series three it already feels like the new character of Foggy Dewhurst has always been in the show.

(468) The 1989 Christmas special What's Santa Brought for Nora Then? contains some Easter eggs which hint that Foggy Dewhurst will soon be returning to the show - which indeed he was.

(469) A lot of cast members in First of the Summer Wine said they tried not to do a direct impersonation of the corresponding actor in Last of the Summer Wine because they were playing their respective character as a young person and no one is the same as a teenager as they are 40 years later. Well, maybe apart from Compo! Compo never really grew up at all.

(470) Jane Freeman was a very accomplished stage actress and did a lot of plays during her breaks from shooting Last of the Summer Wine.

(471) Seymour came across as quite aloof and strange at first but Roy Clarke and Michael Aldridge soon softened the character. Seymour became very whimsical and sweet and was a nice addition to the show.

(472) In the episode Why Does Norman Clegg Buy Ladies' Elastic Stockings? there is a little music cue riffing on the

American soap opera Dallas (which revolved around Texas oil tycoons) when Compo and Clegg drill for oil.

(473) Robert Fyfe actually appeared in some Hollywood movies when Last of the Summer Ended. He was in Cloud Atlas and Pride and Prejudice and Zombies. Robert also appeared in Coronation Street as Malcom Lagg.

(474) The original concept for the character of Marina is that she was going to be a widow. This was dropped though. Marina instead became a single woman desperate for some love and attention.

(475) One of the main reasons why Michael Aldridge was cast as Seymour, besides being a very fine and respected actor, is that he was different enough from Brian Wilde so as not to draw direct comparisons to Foggy (who was obviously a difficult act to follow).

(476) Alan J W Bell said it was his wife who suggested Thora Hird for the part of Edie. Alan was doubtful that a big star like Thora Hird would agree to take a supporting role in Summer Wine but - happily - Thora was delighted to accept the role of Edie. Thora loved Yorkshire and so the idea of being in Last of the Summer Wine was something that appealed to her.

(477) One of the reasons why Sarah Thomas was cast as Glenda is that she had a resemblance to a younger version of Thora Hird.

(478) Juliette Kaplan said she angrily confronted the BBC One controller Jay Hunt at a dinner when Last of the Summer Wine was axed. Juliette said that Jay Hunt got a bit flustered and was clearly trying to escape!

(479) Barry Wilkinson is always searching for a hobby to make his life more interesting. Before he settled on golf, the hobbies

he tried include kite flying, a radio controlled aeroplane, music instruments, and country & western!

(480) In the final series of Last of the Summer Wine, Pearl throws Howard out but takes him back in the last episode. Despite everything these two people do have a bond - though you wouldn't know it at the best of times!

(481) Roy Clarke said he was quite surprised when Last of the Summer Wine became a huge ratings smash and a mainstream success. He had never anticipated that the show had the potential to be so popular.

(482) Peter Sallis was unavailable for location shooting on First of the Summer Wine because he was obviously still making Last of the Summer Wine. Peter's scenes in the prequel show were nearly all shot in a studio.

(483) Jean Alexander made her debut in Last of the Summer Wine about a year after play Hilda Ogden for the last time in Coronation Street.

(484) Jean Fergusson was something of a rarity in the Summer Wine cast because she was actually born in Yorkshire. Jean was born in Wakefield.

(485) In the episode titled The Treasure of the Deep there is a musical reference during the launderette scene to the Marvin Gaye song I Heard It Through the Grapevine. This a reference to a famous Levi jeans commercial of the era which featured the model Nick Kamen. In the commercial, Kamen stripped to his boxer shorts in a 1950s-style launderette as the song plays.

(486) The top rated episode of Last of the Summer Wine on IMDB is Just a Small Funeral with a rating of 9.

(487) The second highest rated episode of Last of the Summer

Wine on IMDB is Getting Sam Home with a rating of 8.9. Third place is a tie between Elegy for Fallen Wellies and Full Steam Behind. Both of these episodes scored 8.8.

(488) The lowest rated episode of Summer Wine on IMDB is Will Randolph Make a Good Impression? In this 2009 episode, Hobo tries to bring romance to Stella and ends up dressing Randolph up as Zorro. Suffice to say, this episode is definitely not vintage Summer Wine. It only scored 5.7 on IMDB.

(489) Alvin is partial to a bit of al fresco dining. He's always having a cup of tea or breakfast outside of his house.

(490) Nora Batty's maiden name is Nora Renshaw.

(491) Jack Smethurst guest starred in the 1997 episode Deviations with Davenport. In this episode, the trio find a man writing a guide book for walkers. Foggy takes charge and - inevitably - gets them completely lost! Jack Smethurst did many things but was probably best known for the sitcom Love Thy Neighbour.

(492) Thora Hird, Kathy Staff, and Joe Gladwin were all in the 1962 British new wave film A Kind of Loving. Kathy and Joe only had tiny parts in this. The film had a tidy cast because it also included Leonard Rossiter, Alan Bates, and James Bolam.

(493) Before he became a writer, Roy Clarke was a policeman, teacher, salesman and taxi driver. He also spent time in the army.

(494) We hear some interior monologues from the characters in Getting Sam Home - which is certainly novel for Summer Wine.

(495) Peter Sallis once said in an interview that he felt the late John Comer as Sid was one of those actors who didn't realise

how good he was. Peter said he was always impressed at how John delivered his lines in such a natural way.

(496) There was some speculation in the press that Last of the Summer Wine might be coming to an end around the time that Michael Aldridge replaced Brian Wilde in the show. This speculation obviously proved to be very wide of the mark because the show carried on for many more years.

(497) Roy Clarke said in an interview that the characters of Mrs Avery and Babs were a bit misjudged and didn't really work.

(498) Compo is a great lover of ferrets. He even takes them on holiday with him.

(499) Foggy Dewhurst will occasionally go into a trance and blank everything out when he is attempting to think or remember something. It's like a Jedi mind trick!

(500) Seymour seems to like wearing his old headmaster's gown when he is at home. He sometimes can't help reverting back to his headmaster days and treating Cleggy and Compo like schoolboys.

(501) The 2008 episode A Short Introduction to Cooper's Rules is something of a departure because it supplies a larger than usual role for the two police officers - who both have names (Cooper and Walsh) now.

(502) The 2008 episode It's Never Ten Years features clips of Bill Owen as Compo and is framed around Truly and Cleggy remembering Compo on the 10th anniversary of his death (though this episode came out only eight years after the funeral episodes). It's a nice trip down memory lane although one does suspect that this episode was cobbled together at the last minute. The general theory is that they wanted to get in a

Bill Owen tribute episode before the BBC pulled the plug on Last of the Summer Wine.

(503) The 2008 episode Get Out of That, Then is the last one where Clegg and Truly are part of the main cast. They couldn't get insurance for Peter Sallis and Frank Thornton to do outdoor scenes after this.

(504) Jean Fergusson said it was no picnic having to navigate the terrain of rural Yorkshire in Marina's high heels!

(505) At the Summer Wine gift shop in Holmfirth you can buy clotted cream and fudge shortbread in a Last of the Summer Wine themed box.

(506) Last of the Summer Wine would sometimes do some shooting in Brighouse. Brighouse is a town within the metropolitan borough of Calderdale, in West Yorkshire.

(507) Series 27 was the first one to be made in high definition.

(508) Ronnie Hazlehurst died in 2007 after composing the music for all the Summer Wine episodes. His name remained on the credits for the last few years of the show because much of his old music was still used.

(509) Russ Abbot had an incompetent spy character in his old comedy sketch show called Basildon Bond. Roy Clarke apparently once wrote a pilot for a Basildon Bond series called 008 – The Real James Bond. This was clearly the basis for the character of Hobo - or at least Hobo's alleged (and highly unbelievable) background.

(510) During the Summer Wine days, Roy Clarke once went down to London to attend a BBC event. However, the security guard wouldn't let Roy in because his name had been left off the guest list. Rather than explain who he was, Roy simply got in his car and drove back to Yorkshire!

(511) Russ Abbot said he initially considered himself too young to be in Last of the Summer Wine! He took the part anyway.

(512) Last of the Summer Wine was a fixture of Sunday teatime for many years, sandwiched alongside shows like Songs of Praise and The Antiques Roadshow. This might be why some people of a certain age don't have fond memories of it. They perhaps associate Summer Wine with the dull Sundays of their childhood when the shops were shut and there were only a few channels on the telly! These days you have gazillions of channels, streaming, and things like YouTube so you aren't at the mercy of BBC and ITV for your home entertainment in the way that kids of past decades were.

(513) Steven Merchant, who wrote The Office with Ricky Gervais, said in an interview that he was always a big fan of Last of the Summer Wine.

(514) The song "Travelers" by Andrew Prahlow from the video game Outer Wilds definitely sounds a bit like the theme tune to Last of the Summer Wine. It could just be a coincidence.

(515) You can buy Last of the Summer Wine themed posters, t-shirts, and mugs on Amazon.

(516) Roy Clarke once said, only half in jest you suspect, that he thinks one of the reasons why Last of the Summer Wine lasted so long is that BBC often forgot it was still being made! This conjures an image of some bigwig sitting at the Beeb's headquarters in 2005 who mistakenly presumes they'd axed the show in 1985 and had no idea it was still in production up in Yorkshire!

(517) Holmfirth celebrated the 50th anniversary of Summer

Wine with pub crawls, a Captain Clutterbuck's Treasure Hunt, and the chance to be photographed alongside Edie Pegden's red Triumph Herald. Jonathan Linsley and Tommy Cannon were on hand to enjoy the celebrations.

(518) Holmfirth can trace its lineage back to the 13th century.

(519) Roy Clarke said that the show forming around a trio (Hobbo, Entwhistle and Alvin) near the end was a definite nod to the show's roots.

(520) In its later series you can definitely sense that Last of the Summer Wine is groping to find a settled central main cast dynamic like the old days of the 'main trio'. The show (until the arrival of Russ Abbot) seemed to experiment with different dynamics and characters. Much of this was obviously forced on them though by cast members passing on, leaving the show, or not being able to shoot as many scenes as they used to. The show simply had to adjust, change, and cope as best it could.

(521) The interior decor of Clegg's last house in the show is simple, old-fashioned, cosy, and ordinary. It matches the character of Clegg perfectly.

(522) The spatial dynamics of Compo's house don't always make sense when he's looking out of a window. It is probably best not to think about these things too much.

(523) Nora's washing line is over the little walkway that runs past the front of her house. Compo always takes a keen interest in what is on Nora's washing line - much to Nora's disgust and dismay.

(524) Roy Clarke said that although he was fairly relaxed about Summer Wine being axed in 2010, him and the cast and crew would have happily carried on making it if the BBC had wanted it to continue.

(525) Clegg, unlike Foggy and Blamire, never really talks about what happened to him in the war. He does mention being in the army though quite a few times.

(526) It is never really explained why Smiler is working for Auntie Wainwright because he clearly loathes this job and the wages are almost certainly terrible - probably even non-existent from what we know about Auntie Wainwright! Maybe Smiler owed Auntie Wainwright a favour or something?

(527) Roy Clarke said that his favourite sitcom out of the ones he didn't write is Dad's Army.

(528) A 1970 Triumph Herald 13/60 that featured in Last of the Summer Wine as Edie's car sold for £16,500 at an auction in 2021.

(529) Foggy Dewhurst always has a neatly trimmed mustache. His predecessor Blamire also had a tache.

(530) Roy Clarke said in a 2018 interview that he enjoys watching Last of the Summer Wine repeats.

(531) Believe it or not, Corgi made a Last of the Summer Wine Land Rover (a reference to Wesley) toy car and Compo figure. Compo is in an out of control armchair! Sadly, you get no Wesley figure in the car though.

(532) Lynda Baron was a guest star in Getting Sam Home. Lynda, famously, was Nurse Gladys Emmanuel in Roy Clarke's Open All Hours. Trivia that'll probably be of no use to you - Lynda was in two Woody Allen films. Scoop and You Will Meet a Tall Dark Stranger.

(533) Open All Hours only ran to four series - which stretched out over nine years. This was due to the fact that Roy was doing Last of the Summer Wine and Ronnie Barker also had other commitments.

(534) Roy Clarke said he doesn't really have a favourite episode of Last of the Summer Wine because he can't even remember half of them now!

(535) Barry has a lot of different cars over the course of Last of the Summer Wine. They surely can't be company cars either because he works in a building society!

(536) Wally Batty made his first appearance in the episode titled Some Enchanted Evening.

(537) Edie has a bit of OCD when it comes to constantly checking that she's locked her front door when leaving the house. I do this too!

(538) Edie putting on a posh voice in Last of the Summer Wine to call Wesley in was dampened down a bit in the end so as not to draw comparisons between Edie and Hyacinth Bucket in Keeping Up Appearances. Speaking for myself, I'd much rather live next door to Edie than Hyacinth Bucket!

(539) Michael Bates served with the Chindits in World War 2. The Chindits were special forces brigades sent behind Japanese lines in Burma. They were commanded by Major General Orde Charles Wingate. Wingate was an adventurer who was an expert in guerilla warfare and rather like the 'troubleshooter' of the British Empire - someone to be sent for whenever there was trouble.

(540) A chair that was used by both Bill and Tom Owen on the set of Last of the Summer Wine was put up for auction recently. Bill used this chair to sit between takes during his last years on Summer Wine and Tom carried on using the chair in honour of his father.

(541) Tom Owen had more or less retired from acting when he was asked to played Compo's son in Last of the Summer Wine. Tom said it didn't take him long to make up his mind and agree to join the show.

(542) Danbury Mint have done little replica's of Nora Batty's house and also the row of houses where Cleggy and Howard and Pearl live. These little models are often for sale on eBay.

(543) Danbury Mint did a Foggy Dewhurst figurine. This figurine can go for £250 on eBay. Danbury Mint have also done figurines for Clegg, Truly, Wally Batty, and Auntie Wainwright.

(544) Barbara Young, who played Stella, was perhaps most celebrated in her career for playing the future Emperor Nero's mother, Agrippina, in the landmark 1976 BBC serial I, Claudius.

(545) Jane Freeman was born Shirley Ann Pithers.

(546) June Whitfield was made a Dame in 2017 for her services to drama and entertainment.

(547) In the 2003 episode The Secret Birthday of Norman Clegg, Cleggy wants to have a quiet birthday lunch with Truly but things don't quite go according to plan. Clegg doesn't reveal how old he is in the episode but Peter Sallis was 82 at the time so we can presume that's more or less what Clegg is too.

(548) Tom Owen was the Head of Drama at Thames Valley University at one point.

(549) Ivy seems to have a slight obsession with stacking scones neatly!

(550) Ivy mostly has green checked drapes in the cafe. She seems to like light blue cups too.

(551) We see a photograph of Truly's ex-wife Mabel (the former Mrs Truelove) in one episode but only from the back.

(552) Having characters mentioned but not seen is a common device in Roy Clarke's work. In his show Open All Hours, we never actually see the mother of Nurse Gladys Emmanuel - though she is (much to the annoyance of Arkwright) still a looming presence in the show. There are a host of characters in Summer Wine who are mentioned but never seen. Roy Clarke said that it works better if you have to imagine some of the characters for yourself. Other shows do this too. In the classic detective series Columbo, Peter Falk's title character frequently mentions his wife but we never actually meet or see her. In the sitcom One Foot in the Grave, Victor Meldrew's cheerful and kind but strange neighbour Nick Swainey has a bedridden mother who he is often talking to. We never actually see Mr Swainey's mother though in the show.

(553) Bill Owen and Kathy Staff were much sought after for panto season during Summer Wine's glory years.

(554) Joe Gladwin began his career in the music halls. It was apparently a tough time for people like Joe when the music hall tradition waned and vanished because they no longer had steady work. Joe was fortunate enough though to forge a television career in the end.

(555) Robert Fyfe said shooting Summer Wine could be hard work because they often had to shoot multiple scenes one after another in location spots. If a film crew have lugged their equipment to a bridge or canal you want to shoot as many scenes as you can there to save money.

(556) Roy Clarke clearly loved Kathy Staff as an actor because she was also in Open All Hours as Mrs Blewitt.

(557) Kathy Staff was named Yorkshire Woman of the Year in 2001. The men's award went to Patrick Stewart - or Captain Picard as he's better known.

(558) You probably won't be surprised to learn that Edie failed her driving test several times!

(559) Peter Sallis said that he barely got to know Holmfirth during production on the early series because he stayed in Marsden. Marsden is a large village in the Colne Valle. Peter said he later rented a cottage in Holmfirth and got to know the place much better.

(560) Peter Sallis said that Holmfirth changed quite a bit during his time on Summer Wine. Peter said it was quieter with far less shops back in 1973.

(561) The character of Wesley Pegden was a clever creation for the show because Wesley's mechanic and inventor status supplied unlimited potential when it came to the plots.

(562) Juliette Kaplan said she wore thermal underwear shooting Summer Wine because it could get a bit nippy in Yorkshire - even in the summer.

(563) Before the Compo funeral episodes aired, Frank Thornton said - "Roy Clarke wrote what they called the Compo Requiem. Encompassing death in a sitcom is almost unheard of.

There's all the poignancy of us losing a friend and at the same time it's very funny. It's most extraordinary stuff. And for

Peter and me, behind the death of Compo was the death of Bill - that could have been so tasteless in the hands of someone else but there won't be a dry eye in the house."

(564) Jean Alexander described Auntie Wainwright as being a bit like a snappy little Yorkshire terrier!

(565) Years after she left the show, Julie T. Wallace said she didn't like her Mrs Avery character in Summer Wine very much. It is probably safe to say that Mrs Avery wouldn't sit at a top table of the greatest Roy Clarke characters.

(566) When she left Last of the Summer Wine to join the revamped Crossroads (though happily Kathy would come back to Summer Wine in the end), Kathy Staff said - "As far as I was concerned, it didn't work last year, so I decided not to do any more. I did feel I had come to the end of the road once Compo had died." Roy Clarke, ever the gentleman, was very sympathetic to Kathy at the time. Roy said he understood why Kathy would feel it wasn't the same without Bill Owen and would respect any decision she made.

(567) Kathy Staff didn't stay in the revamped Crossroads for long and quit fairly soon - which opened the door to a Summer Wine return. Kathy, who was a very religious lady, felt the new version of Crossroads was too risqué and modern for her liking and not her cup of tea. "It wasn't the Crossroads I was in originally. That was a really happy family show and anybody could watch. I was a bit disappointed when I got in and saw the scripts and the storylines. You've got a girl of 16 pregnant right away and, I mean, she didn't really know who the father was, which makes it even worse."

(568) When he joined Last of the Summer Wine, Tom Owen was active in the local community in Holmfirth because this is something his father was famous for. Tom wanted to continue the good work of his father.

(569) In 2023 it was reported in the media that Holmfirth had been named one of the best places in Britain to go for a little holiday break. Other places named included Blaenau Ffestiniog in North Wales, various spots in Cumbria, and Staithes. Staithes is a seaside village in North Yorkshire.

(570) Bill Owen was raised in the London district of South Acton.

(571) Peter Sallis was in the film Saturday Night and Sunday Morning. Saturday Night and Sunday Morning is a classic British 'social realist' film from 1960 directed by Karel Reisz. There were actually three other actors in this film who ended up appearing in Last of the Summer Wine - Shirley Anne Field, Bryan Pringle, and Jack Smethurst.

(572) No one in Last of the Summer Wine could understand why Compo was attracted to Nora Batty - not even Compo himself!

(573) Frank Thornton said that it was only when he joined the cast of Last of the Summer Wine that he remembered he had done a television play many decades ago called Father of the Bride which was written by Roy Clarke.

(574) Stephen Lewis said of playing Smiler in Last of the Summer Wine - "It's not work at all. It is lovely to be associated with a programme like this, with such wonderful people. When you can give laughter to so many people in a world that is so often full of misery, then it has to be worthwhile."

(575) Herbert Truelove wears a trilby hat.

(576) When the show was in production, cast members from Summer Wine would often be asked to turn on the Christmas lights in Holmfirth.

(577) Michael Bates made his last appearance as Blamire in the April 1975 episode Northern Flying Circus.

(578) In the pilot episode, Clegg is cycling to the church and hitches a ride by holding onto a hearse. You couldn't imagine the Cleggy of later seasons doing that!

(579) Robert Lang was a guest star in the episode The Flag & Further Snags. Robert Lang was in literally everything on television in his long career. He was also in films like Four Weddings and a Funeral, The House That Dripped Blood, Wilde, and The First Great Train Robbery.

(580) Alan J W Bell said that Dame Thora Hird was the greatest actress he ever worked with.

(581) There is no real reason given in the show for why Crusher Milburn has vanished after the departure of Jonathan Linsley.

(582) Roy Clarke said he sometimes used to look through telephone directories trying to find the right name for a character.

(583) John Dair had a small role in the pub scene in Here We Go into The Wild Blue Yonder. John Dair was in many things, including big films, but he was probably best known for playing Crusher - the hefty bodyguard of Harry Grout in Porridge. John was also in the Nick Kamen advert for Levi that Summer Wine riffed on.

(584) Roy Clarke said that when was asked to write First of the Summer Wine he didn't have any backstory at all for the Last of the Summer Wine characters when they were younger. He simply had to make one up for the prequel and hope that it meshed fairly well.

(585) Truly's background as 'Truly of the Yard' doesn't seem to cut much ice with the police officers in Last of the Summer Wine. They've never heard of him!

(586) Most of the cast and crew expected the show to end when Bill Owen passed away. It obviously managed to keep going for quite a while though.

(587) Robert Fyfe said that when he joined the cast of Summer Wine as Howard he only expected the job to last for a few years because he presumed the show would run its course soon and be retired by the BBC. He ended up in it for 25 years!

(588) Juliette Kaplan and Jean Ferguson, who played rivals Pearl and Marina, were very good friends in real life and had known each other for years. Juliette and Jean would often get a cup of tea together in Holmfirth while shooting Summer Wine - which caused a few double takes among the public!

(589) Juliette Kaplan said she was absolutely nothing like Pearl in real life but did add that her children might not agree with that!

(590) In the episode Return of the Warrior, Seymour expresses surprise that caning has been banned in schools. However, Seymour had already pointed this out in an earlier episode. This is what you might describe as a slight continuity goof.

(591) Burt Kwouk was in three James Bond films - Goldfinger, You Only Live Twice, and Casino Royale. 1967's Casino Royale was a comedy spoof that had nothing to do with Cubby Broccoli/Harry Saltzman and their 'official' series featuring Sean Connery. Someone else owned the rights to Casino Royale at the time.

(592) In the looks department, Truly compares his former wife to the old comedian Max Wall! That's not very flattering!

(593) Tom Owen said that he never tried to copy his father's performance when he played Tom Simmonite because his father was an impossible act to follow. Tom said he tried to make his character very different from Compo.

(594) A developer named Gleeson Homes was fined £9,000 in Holmfirth 2002 for felling two trees which sat out the back of the house used as Nora Batty's home in the show. These trees were often seen in the show until Gleeson Homes (that name sounds like a Summer Wine character!) had them cut down. Homes thought he had permission but it turned out he didn't and so he got into trouble. Mr Homes was apparently renovating a mill. The trees sat in a conservation area so no one had a right to cut them down.

(595) The scenes where Tom Simmonite takes refuge in an allotment shed to hide from the repo man were shot at Brooklands Nurseries in Holmirth. Some old sheds and chicken wire was added to a little spot to make it look like an allotment.

(596) Foggy's 'ladyfriend' in Who Made a Bit of a Splash in Wales Then? was played by Margaret John. Margaret had a long career - including cult TV like Doctor Who and Doomwatch. Later in her career she appeared in comedy shows like The Mighty Boosh and Little Britain. The last thing Margaret did was two episodes of Game of Thrones in 2011.

(597) The Christmas special What's Santa Brought for Nora Then? was the last full length appearance by Michael Aldridge as Seymour. He does make a welcome cameo in Return of the Warrior though.

(598) When he was told in 2003 that a Radio Times poll had voted Summer Wine as the show most people wanted axed, Roy Clarke said - "I don't see why it should finish. If people don't like it they shouldn't switch it on! What's the matter?

Are they too idle to turn it off?"

(599) Truly claims that when he was in the police he once captured a famous serial killer. This detail veers him slightly into Foggy Dewhurst style tall tales territory but who knows? Maybe he really did capture a serial killer.

(600) Pete Postlethwaite made a brief appearance in the 1979 episode A Merry Heatwave. Pete Postlethwaite would go on to become a highly acclaimed actor. He also appeared in big Hollywood films.

(601) Stephen Lewis said he got fan mail from all around the world when he became a regular as Smiler in Summer Wine. "I get fan mail every day, some from all over the world. Summer Wine seems to have an appeal to people in so many countries and of so many ages. I think it's because there's something special about British humour."

(602) June Whitfield said that thanks to Absolutely Fabulous and Last of the Summer Wine her career later in life became busier than it had been since the 1950s!

(603) When he joined the cast of Last of the Summer Wine as Herbert Truelove, Frank Thornton said - "That's the lovely thing about being an actor; they don't want old dancers, they don't want old singers but there's always something for old actors. How many people at my age can get a job as good as this one?"

(604) Peter Sallis said he rather enjoyed Last of the Summer Wine becoming more of an ensemble because it meant he had to do less work!

(605) The librarian Lucinda Davenport is a bit atypical for a Last of the Summer Wine woman because she's sensitive and friendly!

(606) Bill Owen said he felt very lucky and grateful for the part of Compo because it gave him a fame and adulation he'd never experienced before.

(607) In the episode Leaving Home Forever, or Till Teatime, we learn that Pearl makes a very good steak and kidney pie. In fact, it may be the only reason why Howard actually stays married to her!

(608) Peter Baldwin was a guest star in the 2009 episode Goodnight Sweet Ferret. Peter was a familiar face to television audiences after playing Derek Wilton in Coronation Street.

(609) When they were shooting Last of the Summer Wine, they would occasionally notice that Peter Sallis was missing and then - after a search - find him idly browsing in a bookshop!

(610) Despite being known as 'Crusher' to everyone, Ivy always insists on calling him Milburn.

(611) In 2004, a Yorkshire haulage firm named new trucks Compo, Cleggy, Seymour, Nora and Foggy in tribute to Last of the Summer Wine!

(612) In a 2005 poll, Thora Hird was named Britain's seventh greatest ever actress. Just in case you are curious, the six people ahead of Thora in the poll were Judi Dench, Julie Walters, Elizabeth Taylor, Helen Mirren, Julie Andrews, and Maggie Smith.

(613) Juliette Kaplan often wore a turban as Peal to keep her pesky character wig in place.

(614) After Bill Owen died, there were plans to have a statue of him in character as Compo in Holmfirth but funding issues frustrated the project. Summer Wine fans eventually raised enough money for a 9 ft stone tribute to Compo but unfortunately planning obstacles once again frustrated the project. Ken Kitson said that in his view there should be a statue of Compo, Clegg, and Foggy together placed outside Sid's Cafe. That sounds like a good idea to me!

(615) Tom Owen's 1991 cameo in Situations Vacant is as a man getting money out of a cash machine who is spooked by Foggy surprising him. Foggy claims that the cash machine gave flashbacks to a pillbox! A pillbox is a type of blockhouse, or concrete dug-in guard-post, often camouflaged, normally equipped with loopholes through which defenders can fire weapons. Pillboxes were obviously used in World War 2.

(616) The Yorkshire Post reported in 2013 that an American fan named Darin Iscrupe created a replica of Sid and Ivy's cafe at his home in Florida!

(617) Seymour had his own correspondence course - the Utterthwaite Postal University.

(618) Blamire thinks he can play the piano though in reality he can't - at least not very well.

(619) Compo's catchphrase, which was triggered by the suspicion that Seymour or Foggy had him in mind for some crazy plan, was - "He's looking at me, Norm! Why's he looking at me, Norm?"

(620) Jane Freeman said that Getting Sam Home was her favourite episode (or film in this case) of Last of the Summer Wine.

(621) Kathy Staff was 42 when she first played Nora Batty.

(622) The father of Julie T. Wallace was the actor Andrew Keir. Andrew Keir played Professor Bernard Quatermass in the

classic Hammer film Quatermass and the Pit.

(623) Brian Wilde's son said that Brian didn't have a favourite out of Porridge and Last of the Summer Wine. He was just grateful to have been in two shows that become very beloved.

(624) Julie T. Wallace told the Daily Mail that while she liked the cast and crew, she left Last of the Summer Wine because she didn't like the director. The person she is talking about is obviously Alan J W Bell.

(625) Brian Wilde described his character Foggy Dewhurst as pompous but harmless. I'm not sure Compo would have agreed that Foggy was harmless!

(626) Roz Utterthwaite was never previously mentioned in Summer Wine until Dora Bryan joined the show.

(627) When he sadly passed away, The Times wrote of Michael Aldridge - 'If Aldridge joined the cast of a show, it invariably meant the injection of an extra dimension of dramatic interest, however modest his role in it. In everything he did, if never a big name, he was a professional to his fingertips.'

(628) Smiler's wife left him to go to Australia.

(629) It is very difficult to find any interviews with Keith Clifford - who played Billy Hardcastle. He did a brief one with a Yorkshire paper when he first became a regular in Summer Wine. Keith said in the interview he'd developed a good chemistry and understanding with Peter Sallis and Frank Thornton and also said it was quite daunting to think he was filling the gap in the trio left by Bill Owen.

(630) Watching the post Compo episodes of Last of the Summer Wine you do get the impression that the show doesn't know exactly what it wants to do with Tom Simmonite. Tom doesn't strike you as a character that was thought out very well.

(631) Peter Sallis said of making the Compo funeral episodes - "It was very moving - it was difficult to know whether I was thinking about Compo or about Bill but I was really thinking about both."

(632) Last of the Summer began the same year that Britain joined the EEC. The European Economic Community would later become the European Union.

(633) Eric Sykes was 83 when he appeared in Last of the Summer Wine. Alan J W Bell said that Eric was sharp as a tack and word perfect.

(634) Holmfirth is sometimes known as Summer Wine Land due to its association with the beloved show.

(635) Other guest stars in Last of the Summer Wine have included Anita Dobson, Hywel Bennett, Jean Boht, Lionel Bart, Matthew Kelly, Norman Rossington, and Roy Hudd.

(636) Jane Freeman said she was happy for shooting to end on the Last of the Summer Wine pilot because she was waiting to go on her honeymoon!

(637) Wesley Pegden certainly proved his worth to the main trio in Last of the Summer Wine. One time he even had to cut Compo out of some bed springs!

(638) Roy Clarke said he found that writing Last of the Summer Wine became easier over time. It became his comfort zone.

(639) Some of the cast (which was considerably smaller back then) stayed at the Coach and Horses at Marsden very early in the show. Roy Clarke said this pub actually had a stripper performing at the weekend!

(640) Edie is clearly very proud of having Seymour as a brother because he is a former headmaster and very clever. It's safe to say that Wesley isn't quite so impressed by Seymour!

(641) Howard is sometimes frustrated by his lack of height - which is (ahem) heightened when he compares himself to Smiler. In real life, Smiler actor Stephen Lewis was 6'1 while Howard actor Robert Fyfe was 5'6.

(642) Many of the cast of First Of The Summer Wine said they were rather upset and disappointed when the show was cancelled after only two series.

(643) The Christmas special Crums is notable because it has a scene where Ivy and Nora talk about their late husbands Sid and Wally and how they miss them. Jane Freeman and Kathy Staff both desired more scenes like this because they wanted Sid and Wally to be audibly missed and remembered - thus keeping the memory of John Comer and Joe Gladwin alive in the show. Jane and Kathy didn't like the thought of Sid and Wally just being forgotten and never mentioned again.

(644) Peter Sallis said that in real life he wasn't much of a fan of hills, dales, and country rambles. He was more of a city person.

(645) According to Jane Freeman, the character of Ivy was sort of based on Roy Clarke's wife!

(646) Kathy Staff said she was rarely recognised in real life because she looked nothing like Nora Batty without the costume and curlers.

(647) Sarah Thomas once said in an interview that there were many reasons why Summer Wine was so enduring and successful but perhaps the most important one was that it was a show that never offends and can be watched by all the family.

(648) Bill Owen once appeared on stage with Katharine Hepburn in As You Like It.

(649) Tom Owen said that joining the cast of Last of the Summer Wine felt a bit like coming home.

(650) Bill Owen once did 'An Evening With Bill Owen' at Holmfirth Civic Hall to raise money towards the River Holme improvement scheme.

(651) Roy Clarke said that on the first six or seven years of Last of the Summer Wine he kept expecting the show to end soon. Before he knew it though the show had been running for decades!

(652) Marina is fond of Tiger Lily perfume.

(653) Robert Fyfe said he enjoyed playing Howard and tried to inject a few little traits and quirks of his own into the character.

(654) Alan J W Bell was once asked if he felt like his career had stalled by spending so many years on Last of the Summer Wine. Alan responded to this by saying - "I joined Last Of The Summer Wine in 1981 and have never regretted it. People say I became stuck in a rut - but what a wonderful rut in which to be stuck!"

(655) A series of Last of the Summer Wine would typically take about four weeks to get all the location work in the can. That was only half the show though because the interiors would then have to be done.

(656) The intro song over the credits of First Of The Summer Wine is Al Bowlly's Sweet And Lovely. Albert Allick Bowlly was a vocalist and jazz guitarist who was popular in Britain. He was killed in 1941 during the Blitz on London.

(657) The relationship between Last of the Summer Wine and Holmfirth has not always run smoothly. Circa 2005, Alan J W Bell complained that compensation demands for inconvenience at shooting locations were occasionally preposterous and liable to bankrupt the show. The specific issue at the time was believed to be use of the house used as Nora Batty's home. Alan threatened that they might have to make Nora move house in the show!

(658) Alan J W Bell directed some episodes of the enjoyable Michael Palin comedy show Ripping Yarns.

(659) The dubbing of John Comer in Getting Sam Home is very well done. It is not jarringly obvious in the film that John is being dubbed.

(660) One of the good things about Last of the Summer Wine is that you can just jump into it at any point and start watching. The vast majority of the episodes are self-contained.

(661) Many of the Summer Wine cast members based in London said that going to Yorkshire to shoot Last of the Summer Wine was a bit like going on holiday!

(662) You could argue that First Of The Summer Wine was a bit ahead of its time because prequels are all the rage now!

(663) Brian Wilde said the worst thing about doing Last of the Summer Wine were the gales that whipped up on the hills. Brian did say though that he enjoyed the Yorkshire countryside.

(664) There were only thirteen episodes of First Of The Summer Wine.

(665) In the prequel show First Of The Summer Wine, a young woman named Anita Pilsworth is keen on Cleggy. Anita is played Linda Davidson - Mary the punk from Eastenders!

(666) Bill Owen said he spent so much time in Yorkshire shooting Last of the Summer Wine that he developed a love of brass band music!

(667) Louis Emerick came third in the 2008 series of Celebrity Master Chef.

(668) Foggy has been known to put customers off their food in Ivy's cafe with his tales of things he had to eat in the jungle!

(669) Tony Capstick, who played the 'second police officer' in Summer Wine, was a presenter on BBC Radio Sheffield for many years.

(670) Julie T. Wallace has been in big films like The Fifth Element and Speed Racer.

(671) Danny O'Dea, who played Eli, was another member of the cast not originally from Yorkshire. Danny was born in Sussex.

(672) Bill Owen and Kathy Staff once appeared as their Summer Wine characters on Noel's House Party. This was a Saturday evening light entertainment show with Noel Edmonds.

(673) Crusher has a Walkman in Last of the Summer Wine. Most young people in the 1980s had a Walkman to listen to music cassettes.

(674) Alan J W Bell once said that, in his experience, comedy is a lot more difficult to do than drama.

(675) Dora Bryan won the Laurence Oliver Award for Best Actress for her performance in the Harold Pinter play The Birthday Party.

(676) In real life, Holmfirth is not quite as serene and peaceful as it looks in Summer Wine. You'll encounter more cars in the town than you ever saw in the show.

(677) Dora Bryan and her husband used to own the Clarges Hotel at 115–119 Marine Parade, Brighton. This hotel was used in the films Carry On Girls and Carry On at Your Convenience. June Whitfield was in Carry On Girls.

(678) In the old music hall days, Wally Batty star Joe Gladwin used to do a comic skit where he pretended to be the world's greatest strongman!

(679) Some fans felt the addition of Reggie Unsworth in the funeral episodes was slightly implausible and didn't quite mesh with the show because we now had to believe that all through Summer Wine the character of Compo had this secret sexy woman he was going to meet each week.

(680) Juliette Kaplan said that when she was first contacted for the part of Peal, the character was described to her as requiring a 'feisty and aggressive' performance.

(681) When Jean Alexander passed away, the local community in Southport said she was a very kind and generous lady who was much loved in the area. One man told the local newspaper that he used to deliver Jean's newspapers and she would give him mince pies and sherry at Christmas as a thank you. You can't imagine Auntie Wainwright doing that!

(682) Pearl always wore wire-rimmed spectacles.

(683) Jonathan Linsley said he became good friends with Bill Owen when he played Crusher in Last of the Summer Wine. Compo and Crusher get on well in the show too.

(684) In the Summer Wine episode Who's That Bloke With Nora Batty Then?, Edie answers the phone and puts on a posh voice to say - "Pegden residence, the lady of the house speaking." This is definitely something that Roy Clarke recycled for Hyacinth Bucket.

(685) Peter Sallis and Bill Owen both trod the boards and did some sterling stage work in plays when their schedule on Summer Wine gave them time.

(686) Mike Grady has done the 'medical television treble' in that he was in Holby City, Casualty, and Doctors!

(687) There is a memorial a bench at Southport Flower Show dedicated to Jean Alexander. Jean was a frequent visitor to the show.

(688) Alan J W Bell apparently played a big part in comic stunts becoming a staple of Summer Wine because he judged that this would give the show broader appeal.

(689) Jean Fergusson was only about 40 when she was cast as Marina in Last of the Summer Wine. Jean had her free bus pass by the time it ended. Despite this, Howard usually referred to her as 'the young lady'!

(690) Last of the Summer Wine sometimes used to beat Eastenders in the ratings in the 1980s. It was hugely popular in those years.

(691) Compo occasionally calls Blamire a 'poof' in the very early episodes when they have an argument. This is obviously something which would be offensive and unacceptable today but in those days it was fairly common for this word to be used in sitcoms as an insult. This word is even used in shows like Only Fools and Horses and Just Good Friends in the 1980s.

(692) You can always tell if someone who hasn't really watched Last of the Summer Wine because they usually describe the show as being about old men going down a hill on a tea tray or in a bath. Sure, there were comic stunts in the show but there was much more to Summer Wine than that. The great lines from Roy Clarke, Cleggy's strange and wonderful philosophical musings, timeless comic performances from the likes of Brian Wilde and Bill Owen, and poignant moments of reflection. If these people missed the more subtle stuff in Last of the Summer Wine or never actually watched the show in the first place that's their loss.

(693) Barbara Young (who played Stella in Summer Wine) was in 60 episodes of Coronation Street in various roles. Despite her acclaimed work on stage and in other television, the newspapers inevitably had 'Coronation Street Star Dies' as their headline in articles about Barbara's passing. Barbara was 92 when she died so she had a pretty good innings.

(694) In addition to serving customers in the cafe, we see in some episodes that Ivy also does outside catering. Given that the cafe often seems to have few customers this perhaps explains how Ivy manages to make ends meet and turn a profit.

(695) On joining the cast of Last of the Summer Wine, Tom Owen said - "Despite my experience in the profession, nothing could prepare me for this new role. Not only was I replacing my father's definitive role as Compo, playing his son but I was about to work on a world renown comedy and be judged by a huge audience of die hard fans. I ignored any reservations that I might have had and went for it. It was only as I was about to walk on set for the first time that the enormity of the task in hand hit me. How could I step onto Dad's patch; what would established actors like Peter Sallis and Thora Hird think of me and could I ever live up to the memory of my Dad?"

(696) Alan J W Bell said that occasionally they would have to alter or axe a scene from Roy Clarke's scripts because Roy had written a set-piece that was too expensive or impractical to shoot.

(697) Julie T. Wallace's full name is Julie Therese Wallace.

(698) It is suggested in the show that Marina lives with her mother and Marina's mother does not like men coming round the house. This would explain why Howard and Marina are always meeting in remote rural spots - rather than just go to Marina's house.

(699) Julie T. Wallace is 6'2 tall. No wonder she towered over Tom Simmonite!

(700) June Whitfield as Nelly was not in the last ever episode.

(701) The Summer Wine stage play's plot revolved around Cleggy having to help Howard out of a mess. This would soon be a common plot in the television show too!

(702) Burt Kwouk's full name was Herbert Tsangtse Kwouk.

(703) Many members of the Summer Wine cast did panto. Bill Owen and Kathy Staff did several and Juliette Kaplan, Jean Fergusson, Dora Byran, Brian Murphy, Sarah Thomas, and others all did quite a few. Peter Sallis and Brian Wilde both only did one so presumably must have decided it wasn't their cup of tea.

(704) Jonathan Linsley said that when he played Crusher in Last of the Summer Wine he actually went to a few nightclubs with Peter Sallis! You can't imagine Cleggy at a nightclub!

(705) In the Last of the Summer Wine stage play from 1983, Foggy's absence (Brian Wilde didn't want to do the play) is explained by him being 'upstairs' with a bad back.

(706) Peter Sallis and Bill Owen apparently did some extra writing on the Summer Wine stage play script by Roy Clarke. Roy Clarke wasn't really involved in the production so he probably wasn't aware of this.

(707) The reviews for the 1983 Summer Wine stage play were pretty decent - although the reviews seemed to suggest it lacked the charm of the television show. The stage play had to be a bit more of a farce than the television show.

(708) There is some very moving acting from Kathy Staff in Elegy For Fallen Wellies. The touching scene where Nora and Ivy talk in Nora's kitchen after Compo's death is beautifully played by Kathy and Jane Freeman.

(709) The Summer Wine stage play performed in 1983 was - sadly - not filmed. Therefore you won't find it on YouTube.

(710) Compo's trousers, as Foggy often reminds us, are frequently on the verge of falling apart.

(711) Bill Owen's full name was William John Owen Rowbotham.

(712) Ivy is a bit of an eavesdropper. She is always trying to overhear what Foggy, Clegg, and Compo are talking about in

the cafe.

(713) Following a week at the Theatre Royal in Nottingham, the Last of the Summer Wine stage show with (among others) Bill Owen and Peter Sallis went on to enjoy a successful summer season at the Pier Theatre Bournemouth. It also ran in Eastbourne and Middlesex.

(714) Roy Clarke said that the reason why the BBC didn't end the show when Bill Owen died is that half a series with Bill was in the can so it would have been a huge loss of money to just leave these episodes sitting on a shelf. Thankfully, Roy was able to write the moving funeral episodes.

(715) A year before joining Last of the Summer Wine, Burt Kwouk was in the film Kiss of the Dragon with the martial arts star Jet Li.

(716) Peter Sallis appeared in Doctor Who in 1967. Patrick Troughton was the Doctor at the time.

(717) Roy Clarke gives Clegg a lovely line in the Compo funeral episodes when Cleggy says that paradise is a place where the sun only comes up when you are awake.

(718) Brian Wilde's son Andrew was the film editor on Last of the Summer Wine from the mid-1990s until the final episode in 2010.

(719) Compo is pretty indestructible in the show. Her performs stunts that James Bond would baulk at and yet never picks up so much as a scratch!

(720) The character of Crusher Milburn was another that was originally conceived for the stage show.

(721) Last of the Summer Wine was quite expensive to make

because they obviously had to send a film crew to do extensive outdoor shooting in Yorkshire.

(722) Another insult Compo likes is to call someone a 'prune'.

(723) The main trio in Last of the Summer (which was Brian, Bill, and Peter at the time) once filmed a skit as Foggy, Compo, and Clegg for the Val Doonican Christmas show. It was never aired though because Roy Clarke found out and refused to let someone else write lines for these characters.

(724) Compo loves splashing in puddles.

(725) Compo can't resist a wall. If he finds one he'll walk along it.

(726) Brian Wilde apparently negotiated a deal where he got more money than Bill Owen and Peter Sallis on Last of the Summer Wine. One would imagine Bill and Peter were not too happy about this.

(727) There is a bit of Compo in Alvin in that Alvin likes to have fun and can be quite childish. Generally though Alvin is more sensible and organised than Compo.

(728) The cast of Last of the Summer Wine would typically rehearse for a week before taping.

(729) Like Blamire and Foggy before them, both Billy and Alvin had a tache.

(730) Jane Freeman and Kathy Staff became good friends in real life while playing Nora and Ivy.

(731) Foggy often wore a scarf when he first entered the show.

(732) Bill Owen's first screen acting credit was in a 1941

Ministry of Information film about a tank patrol lost behind German lines in the desert.

(733) Compo often calls Foggy a 'giraffe' and makes comments about his height. Brian Wilde was apparently 6'3 - so much taller than his co-stars.

(734) Brian Wilde asked for the series eight scripts to be rewritten because he didn't think they were good. The strange thing about this is that most people would say the series eight scripts were terrific. The scripts were obviously not rewritten.

(735) Enwistle's outfit in Summer Wine is a woolly hat and one of those black coats with shoulder patches that binmen used to wear.

(736) Fulton Mackay being contacted as a replacement for Brian Wilde before series eight was a bit of a negotiating tactic. They must have known that word would get to Brian that his Porridge co-star was being lined up as his replacement. Brian did indeed change his mind and come back.

(737) Last of the Summer Wine is a very relaxing show to have on in the background. Seeing the characters is like meeting up with old friends.

(738) Brian Wilde originally planned to leave Last of the Summer Wine both before and after Getting Sam Home but he was persuaded to sign for another series.

(739) In the prequel show First of the Summer Wine, Clegg and Compo don't knock around with Foggy much. Foggy is too busy forging the start of his military career.

(740) Nora Batty was lethal with a broom but she was also pretty deadly with a mop!

(741) Near the end of Last of the Summer Wine, Russ Abbot's Hobo sort of took over the Clegg/Truly role of trying to get Howard out of his various troubles.

(742) Stuart Fell, who was Bill Owen's stunt double as Compo for many episodes, also worked as a stuntman on Doctor Who, Superman, The Empire Strikes Back, and Blake's 7.

(743) Bill Owen said that although he didn't have much in common with Peter Sallis and Brian Wilde offscreen their chemistry in front of the camera was always terrific. Bill was pals with Peter offscreen but not so much with Brian.

(744) Peter Sallis once compared the Last of the Summer Wine theme tune to the composer Elgar.

(745) Barry's hobbies have included amateur dramatics and playing the saxophone. Glenda wouldn't him play the saxophone in the house!

(746) Despite his amazingly prolific output as a writer, Roy Clarke said he didn't consider himself to be a workaholic and always took the evenings off during his career.

(747) In the episode The Most Powerful Eyeballs in West Yorkshire, Foggy somehow manages to hypnotise himself!

(748) Foggy is something of a trainspotter. He is in his element in Full Steam Behind.

(749) At the end of The Black Widow the Summer Wine theme is reconfigured in two-step fashion in light of Foggy being trapped on the dancefloor with Mrs Jack Attercliffe!

(750) In the Blamire years, the tables in Ivy's cafe are tiny and ancient. They look like they are about to fall to pieces!

(751) Gorden Kaye was a guest star in The Last Surviving Maurice Chevalier Impression. Gordon was obviously most famous for playing café owner René Artois in 'Allo 'Allo!.

(752) Alan J W Bell said that Peter Sallis had his own very clear ideas on how the character of Norman Clegg should be played and therefore didn't enjoy being given too much direction.

(753) Bill Owen said he never argued about politics with Brian Wilde - as Bill had done with Michael Bates - because it was a subject that didn't interest Brian.

(754) It is somewhat ironic that the closest thing the BBC have had to a replacement for Last of the Summer Wine on Sunday evenings is Still Open Hours - which is sort of like Roy Clarke's disguised continuation of Summer Wine!

(755) Marina's line "Norman Clegg that was!" is actually a reference to mistaken identity in the stage play.

(756) The Last of the Summer Wine stage version with Bill Owen and Peter Sallis was directed by Jan Butlin. Jan was also a writer and actress.

(757) It is a shame that the health/personal circumstances and passing of Michael Bates and Michael Aldridge meant that they couldn't come back to the show for a few guest appearances after they left. It would have been fun to see Blamire or Seymour interacting with Foggy.

(758) Uncle of the Bride was repeated on the BBC in 1994 as a tribute to Michael Aldridge - who had sadly passed away.

(759) The first influx of new characters in Summer Wine - the first move towards the ensemble - came with the first departure of Foggy. It appears that Roy Clarke wanted to compensate for the loss of Foggy with new characters and a slightly different approach.

(760) Long before Liz Fraser played Compo's 'Thursday woman' Reggie in the Compo funeral trilogy, Liz and Bill Owen acted together in Carry on Regardless in 1961.

(761) When the show began in 1973, the price board in Ivy's cafe lists fish & chips as costing 25p!

(762) The Mike Sammes Singers sang the Summer Wine theme tune at the start of Getting Sam Home.

(763) The Christmas episode Crums has a rather unusual title. Crums is supposed to stand for Christmas Resistance Underground Movement.

(764) Peter Sallis narrated a commercial for Polo mints in 1994. Polo mints without holes no less!

(765) Smiler became a regular character about two years after first appearing in That Certain Smile.

(766) One of Mike Grady's big breaks was doing Pepsi commercials. Mike played a nerdy sort of character in the commercials.

(767) Brian Wilde leaving Summer Wine twice and being a bit unhappy at times is (the theory goes) generally explained by him becoming a bit bored playing the same character all the time. This is fair enough I suppose as actors like to do different things.

(768) Brian Wilde did an advert for Clover butter spread in 1985. Not as Foggy obviously!

(769) The Yorkshire Post once got a letter from someone

named Roger Bates suggesting that Roy Clarke should have a Knighthood. I concur with Mr Bates! He wrote - 'Throughout the coronavirus crisis, episodes, all-be-it repeats, of Last of the Summer Wine have lightened the gloom, and all featuring Holmfirth which, in my view, is one of the most attractive and scenic areas of West Yorkshire. A generous sprinkling of some of the best acting talents have kept us good Yorkshire folk amused and entertained. How about a round of applause for Roy Clarke, who was born in Austerfield, and a knighthood?'

(770) Peter Sallis and Bill Owen had a caravan on the set with separate rooms. This was where they took a nap or read lines between takes.

(771) There was a lot of smoking in the early series of Last of the Summer Wine. This was phased out though after the Blamire years. In one of the Christmas episodes later on, Cleggy mentions that he gave up smoking for health reasons.

(772) Quite a lot of cast members in Summer Wine, like Kathy Staff, John Comer, Brian Wilde, and Joe Gladwin, were from the Manchester area.

(773) The most important piece of equipment in Ivy's cafe is the tea urn. A tea urn is a kettle-like container used for brewing and dispensing large quantities of tea. It typically has a large capacity and is designed to keep the tea hot for an extended period of time. Tea urns are commonly used in catering and hospitality settings, such as restaurants, hotels, and event venues, where there is a need to serve tea to a large number of people.

(774) In the later series of Summer Wine we see a bit more of the back room/kitchen of the cafe.

(775) Jane Freeman was brought up in Wales - though you wouldn't know it watching Summer Wine because Ivy is a

believable Yorkshire lass.

(776) Tom Owen did a one-man show called Last of the Summer Wine – Treading the Boards. The show was about both Tom and his father Bill.

(777) Some of the scripts from Last of the Summer Wine have been sold at auctions.

(778) Tom Owen was in a television film in 1987 called Queenie which starred, among others, Kirk Douglas. Tom was out of work for a time after this and had to claim unemployment benefit. In his one man show Tom said this perfectly sums up the unpredictable nature of the acting industry. One minute you are working with Kirk Douglas and the next minute you are signing on at the Job Centre. Talk about ups and downs!

(779) It is definitely not advisable to do any browsing in Auntie Wainwright's shop. You won't escape without buying anything. And the item you end up with is liable to be completely random and useless. You'll end up with a gorilla suit or gramophone or something!

(780) In the episode The Second Husband and the Showgirls, Glenda wonders aloud why people like Nora and Pearl ever got married given that all they do is complain about men. It's a question we've probably all had ourselves from time to time watching the show!

(781) Peter Sallis once said that he hoped that Last of the Summer Wine would carry on beyond him if he passed away. In the end Peter actually outlived Last of the Summer Wine by several years.

(782) In the 2003 episode The Secret Birthday of Norman Clegg, it is very noticeable that stand ins are being used for

Thora Hird as Edie.

(783) Clegg sometimes seems to have trouble with mothballs in his old suits. Mothballs are small spherical balls which release a strong odour that is toxic to moths and other insects, effectively keeping them away from stored clothing, blankets, or other items that may be susceptible to damage by moths.

(784) In 1994, June Whitfield was given a Lifetime Achievement Award by the British Comedy Awards.

(785) Jean Alexander's real name was Jean Mavis Hodgkinson.

(786) When the show was axed, James Kettle in The Guardian defended Last of the Summer Wine and said he would miss the show. 'What Last of the Summer Wine (and, to be more accurate, its creator and sole writer Roy Clarke) has always been good at is devising well-observed, highly peculiar yet believable characters. There are the obvious legends like the perpetually unimpressed Nora Batty – the preposterous sex symbol clad in wrinkled tights. But there are smaller, subtler gems: Juliette Kaplan's hard-nosed, embittered Pearl is, in her own way, as deft and memorable a representation of elderly northern womanhood as anything dreamed up by Alan Bennett. Although its humour often relies on slapstick, thanks to the calibre of the performers, it's damn good slapstick. There's a tendency to look down on it as a low form of comedy, but through the years, good slapstick (Laurel and Hardy, Basil's attacks on Manuel in Fawlty Towers) has been a reliable source of great entertainment. In any case, getting hung up on the slapstick means you're likely to miss the heart of the programme – a story of people of advanced years messing about in the face of their own mortality, whiling away the time as life winds down.'

(787) Truly likes to call himself Truly of the Yard. We get the impression that Truly exaggerates his police career a little bit -

though nowhere near the extent that Foggy exaggerated his military career.

(788) Danbury Mint did a ceramic Nora Batty figurine. Nora is in her blue cardigan and curlers and - as usual - looking a bit grumpy. Last time I looked this figurine goes for about £70 on eBay.

(789) Tom Owen didn't do much more television or film acting after Last of the Summer Wine ended in 2010. Tom did have small parts in a couple of films though - The Bromley Boys and The Guernsey Literary and Potato Peel Pie Society.

(790) Michael Bates spoke fluent Urdu because he was born in India.

(791) Summer Wine fans tend to be slightly divided on the character of Alvin. Speaking personally, I liked Alvin and have always enjoyed Brian Murphy's comedic roles.

(792) Robert Fyfe played a doctor in the 1982 horror film Xtro. Xtro is a cultishly bizarre (if not terribly good) sci-fi horror film directed by Harry Bromley Davenport.

(793) While there were still a few bright spots here and there, it is probably fair to say some felt that Roy Clarke's writing declined somewhat in the end. Still Open Hours and the later series of Last of the Summer Wine were patently not as good as Roy's older work. It could simply be the case that Roy had written so many scripts he was starting to run out of ideas.

(794) Crusher was a bit more menacing in the stage play. He's more of a gentle giant Forrest Gump type in the TV show.

(795) Amy Shaw was often used as a double for Thora Hird in some of the driving scenes involving Edie.

(796) Although some retrospectives of the show tend to suggest the comedy stunts only began during the Foggy era this is not strictly true. The early Blamire era did have a few comical stunts and at the very least anticipated the direction the show would take in the future.

(797) Last of the Summer Wine is the longest running British sitcom but what is the second longest running British sitcom? Well, that title goes to Not Going Out - which, at the time of writing, has run to thirteen series and nearly a hundred episodes. Occasional Summer Wine star, the late Bobby Ball, was a frequent guest star in Not Going Out.

(798) There is a melancholic quality to Blamire in that we get the genuine sense he's frustrated by his current circumstances and would rather be somewhere else.

(799) Ros Utterthwaite is nothing like her sister Edie. Ros often talks about all the romantic flings she's had - much to Edie's embarrassment!

(800) Russ Abbot said he got fan mail from people of all ages - often kids - when he was in Last of the Summer Wine. Russ said the fan mail from kids was often addressed to his character Hobo!

(801) Last of the Summer Wine was nominated for a BAFTA several times in the best comedy show category.

(802) In the Christmas episode Variations on a Theme of the Widow Winstanley, Clegg is struggling to remember the name of a girl who liked licorice. The person in question turns out to be Audrey Needham - now the Widow Winstanley.

(803) The character of Mrs Avery was only in the show for about a year.

(804) Roy Clarke felt there was a strange plausibility to the character of Foggy. Most of us have met someone who embellishes their background in a faintly ludicrous way so Foggy is a long from being jarringly unrealistic.

(805) Alan J W Bell said that young executives at the BBC had a snooty disdain and dislike for Last of the Summer Wine in its last years. There was no love lost between Alan and elements of the BBC during this time.

(806) Even in its last years, when most would probably agree that the show was not as good as it used to be, Last of the Summer Wine still had that cosy, familiar, comfort blanket sort of feel. For those who fell for its charms, Summer Wine always provided a nice place to escape your troubles for half an hour.

(807) In some of the later series of Last of the Summer Wine you can sometimes detect that in some of the countryside scenes and long shots, Clegg is not Peter Sallis but a body double wearing his costume. This was obviously done to lighten the workload of Peter Sallis. Give him less walking to do!

(808) Compo is fond of using the word 'Herbert' as an insult. 'Herbert' is old working-class slang for a foolish person.

(809) Another insult that Compo is fond of using is to call someone (usually Foggy) a 'pillock'. Pillock is slang for a stupid person.

(810) Another insult that Compo occasionally uses is 'wazzock'. This is slang for someone who is being a bit stupid or idiotic.

(811) Alvin Smedley is very distinctive because he wears his cap back to front.

(812) Brian Murphy was another member of the Summer Wine cast who wasn't from Yorkshire. Brian was born on the Isle of Wight.

(813) Wesley spends most of his time wearing oil stained overalls and a cap. Occasionally he has to smarten himself up and wear a suit and tie for an event like a wedding. Wesley is almost unrecogisable in a suit!

(814) Fans of the show still leave wellies at the grave of Bill Owen.

(815) Although the core premise of Last of the Summer Wine is older people who refuse to act their age, there are some wistful lines by Roy Clarke about the passing of time. In the early series Cleggy comments you don't get to be nineteen for very long. In the Compo funeral trilogy, Cleggy wonders where all the time went and says it doesn't seem like five minutes since they were all at school together.

(816) The secret to Wesley and Edie's marriage is clearly the fact that Wesley spends most of his time at his shed tinkering with cars and engines. If he was in the house all day they'd probably get on each other's nerves!

(817) The Hyde Park Picture House was used in First of the Summer Wine. The Hyde Park Picture House is a cinema and Grade II listed building in the Hyde Park area of Leeds.

(818) Bill Owen and Kathy Staff released a comedy song called Nora Batty's Stockings in 1983. Bill Owen used to be a songwriter in addition to being an actor. This song is easy to find on YouTube.

(819) Stan Richards had a small part in the 1979 Summer Wine episode The Flag and Further Snags. Stan Richards would become a familiar face on television for his role as the

eccentric workshy gamekeeper Seth Richards in the Yorkshire soap opera Emmerdale (which was called Emmerdale Farm in the early days). Believe it or not, Stan was in 1,690 episodes of Emmerdale!

(820) Gordon Wharmby got the part of Wesley because he did an audition for a one-off smaller part as another character and they liked him so much they asked him to come back and read for Wesley.

(821) In the scenes where the characters in Summer Wine are in a pub, non-alcoholic beverages made to look like beer were used. You don't want the cast getting sloshed if you have do several takes!

(822) Sarah Thomas played Enid in Worzel Gummidge several years before the part of Glenda Wilkinson came her way. Worzel Gummidge was a children's drama/comedy that began in 1979. The series was based on the Worzel Gummidge books by Barbara Euphan Todd. It stars former Doctor Who actor Jon Pertwee as Worzel Gummidge, a scarecrow on Scatterbrook Farm. Worzel is no ordinary scarecrow though. He was created by the mysterious Crowman (Geoffrey Bayldon) and it seems that the Crowman's creations were given the gift of life. So daft old Worzel frequently comes to life when no one is around and gets into all manner of comical scrapes. The only people who seem to know he's real are the two children on the farm. Worzel has two all consuming passions. The pursuit of the snooty coconut shy doll Aunt Sally (Una Stubbs) and his great love of cake.

(823) The White Horse in Holmfirth was used a lot when the characters go to the pub. You can visit this pub in real life and there are mementos and photographs from the show on display.

(824) Mike Grady said that, when he shot outdoor scenes in

Last of the Summer Wine, sometimes a member of the public would come up and start chatting to him.

(825) You could make a case for arguing that Howard, in relation to Pearl, has developed Stockholm syndrome! Stockholm syndrome refers to a psychological phenomenon where hostages develop an emotional attachment with their captors, often resulting loyalty towards them.

(826) Jean Fergusson said the part of Marina was described as the 'peroxide town floozy' when she was first offered it.

(827) Wellington boots, so beloved by Compo, are a type of waterproof footwear typically made of rubber. They are named after Arthur Wellesley, the first Duke of Wellington, who popularised the style in the early 19th century. Most people in Britain have owned a pair of 'wellies' - especially as kids.

(828) When Tom Owen sadly passed away, Mike Grady said on social media - 'I am shocked and saddened. Tom Owen was a princely colleague. We worked joyously and hilariously together on Last of the Summer Wine for a number of seasons. I always hoped for a working reunion one day.'

(829) Compo is notoriously bad at picking winners when he's betting on the horses. Cleggy later tells Tom Simmonite that when bookies saw his father coming into their shop it was like seeing Santa coming down the chimney!

(830) Morton Beemish is plainly not a great repo man because not only is he easy to evade he's also quite gullible!

(831) Sid and Ivy's cafe has Beale printed on it some early episodes. It is never confirmed though whether this is their name.

(832) It seems that rather than divorce Howard or kick him out for his numerous dalliances with Marina, Pearl has simply decided to make Howard's life a misery! It could be the case that Pearl's pride wouldn't allow her to become known as the woman who lost her husband to Marina. The comedy in the situation comes from the almost certain knowledge that Howard would never actually leave Peal anyway even if he was given the chance.

(833) We never learn in the show what Marina's surname is.

(834) Ferrets are intelligent and social animals, known for their playful and energetic nature. They require plenty of mental and physical stimulation, such as interactive toys and regular exercise, to prevent boredom. Compo will be well aware of all of this as a ferret owner and lover.

(835) Foggy Dewhurst said that he never married because he follows the code of the Samurai and marriage is not for warriors!

(836) Peter Sallis once said in an interview that the hangliding episodes were among his favourites in Last of the Summer Wine. He was obviously referring to Here We Go Into The Wild Blue Yonder and Here We Go Again Into The Wild Blue Yonder. These episodes are from 1979.

(837) Holmfirth is known for its lovely stone cottages.

(838) The audio format for the last seven years of the show was Dolby Digital.

(839) Reggie Unsworth turned out to be Compo's 'Thursday woman'. The implication in the funeral episodes is that Reggie and Compo could have been more but Compo could never do this because he always held a lingering candle for Nora.

(840) On his Twitter feed a few years ago, Mike Grady commented that it is always a bit strange and bittersweet for him to stumble across a Last of the Summer Wine episode on telly because he is one of the few people in the show who is still alive. When he watches the show now he sees many old friends and colleagues who are no longer around.

(841) Blake Butler, who played the librarian Mr Wainwright, sadly died quite young in 1981. After his stint on Summer Wine he appeared in various shows - including George & Mildred and Rumpole of the Bailey.

(842) Compo was only married to his wife for a few weeks before she did a bunk and left him.

(843) Blake Butler only appeared in five episodes of Last of the Summer Wine as the librarian Mr Wainwright.

(844) Brian Murphy said of his time in Last of the Summer Wine - "The combination of such good scripts, old friends, and wonderful scenery made it a most pleasurable job for the advancing years."

(845) Dora Bryan is billed in the opening credits for The McDonaghs of Jamieson Street but does not actually appear in the episode.

(846) It is said that Brian Wilde preferred Sydney Lotterby to Alan J W Bell on Last of the Summer Wine. This is apparently because Brian preferred the more efficient style (less takes) of Lotterby and the way he would do close up shots of the actors in the rural scenes (Alan, by contrast, loved to get in a long shot of the men walking).

(847) Roy Clarke felt that Last of the Summer Wine having a strangely low-key sort of ending was actually fitting as it was in the spirit of the show.

(848) Norman Clegg is an example of the everyman character. The everyman is a fiction trope where there is one character who is very relatable to the audience and so helps us have empathy with the scenarios depicted. The everyman is sort of like our window into the story. Classic fictional 'everyman' characters include Arthur Dent from The Hitchhiker's Guide to the Galaxy, Bilbo Baggins from The Hobbit, and Tim in The Office. Weirdly, these three characters have all been played by Martin Freeman - so he must be the perfect everyman actor! When we watch Last of the Summer Wine it is the 'everyman' Cleggy who most of us identify with because he is ordinary and also quite sensible and realistic compared to the other characters. Clegg also fufils this function in the prequel show First of the Summer Wine - even supplying narration.

(849) Tom Simmonite always insisted that Mrs Avery was just an 'acquaintance' but Mrs Avery seemed to think it was more than this.

(850) It's a slight shame that, given that both characters are in the episode, they don't have Foggy meeting Seymour in Return of the Warrior. Still, it's a great episode nonetheless. Admittedly, Seymour wasn't in the episode for long anyway.

(851) Alan J W Bell was the man who did The HitchHiker's Guide to the Galaxy television series for the BBC - adapting it from radio. Alan was no fan of science fiction but took the job anyway. Alan said he got flak from fans for the adaptation but if you ask me the bargain basement TV show is a lot better than the dreadful Hollywood film version they later made.

(852) It was noticeable that Entwistle's role in the show seemed to decline as it went on. It could be the case that Burt Kwouk, who was pushing eighty by the end, couldn't do as much filming as he used to.

(853) One of the problems with the last few series of Summer

Wine is that, although there were still some funny episodes and good scenes, there was no one to fill the philosopher role of Clegg (who was hardly in the series now due to the age of Peter Sallis). Entwistle was the closest to this but it obviously wasn't the same. Roy Clarke had used Clegg to inject his own personal voice into the show so this element was missed.

(854) In 1999, Last of the Summer Wine won the National Television Award for Most Popular Comedy Programme.

(855) Brian Murphy was a bit wary of having Alvin be Nora's neighbour in the show because he didn't want his character to feel like a rehash of Compo. In the end the Alvin/Nora scenes were different enough to the Nora/Compo vignettes to assuage Brian's fears that he was being asked to impersonate Bill Owen.

(856) When the show was cancelled and the last ever series was about to begin, Russ Abbot said in the media - "Actually, I'm very disappointed. Not with the BBC as such but with certain people who came in and said 'OK, this is going' and then they went, themselves. To make those kinds of decisions without any consultation with viewers is disgraceful, and that's why there's been such a big hue and cry about it. The most harmful part was the people who axed it didn't give Roy Clarke the respect he deserves by saying 'Roy, we're only going to do one more series - write a fabulous ending'. For Roy to be able to write that many episodes for so long - and then not give him the chance to write an epitaph - I think that's wrong."

(857) When he joined the cast of Last of the Summer Wine, Russ Abbot did an interview on Loose Women and said he'd happily follow in the footsteps of Peter Sallis and Frank Thornton and do the show for years into his old age. The BBC obviously foiled this plan by giving the show the axe shortly afterwards!

(858) Billy Hardcastle is often trying to find new recruits for his band of Merry Men. He isn't very successful in this mission though.

(859) Most (if not all) of the street names you see in Last of the Summer Wine are fictitious.

(860) Billy Hardcastle made his last appearance in Plenty of Room in the Back.

(861) Alvin and Compo have something in common in that they've both had a bash at skateboarding.

(862) At the Summer Wine gift shop in Holmfirth you can buy Last of the Summer Wine themed plates and candles.

(863) Alan J W Bell said there was a very small chain of command on Last of the Summer Wine during his tenure. Alan said he had an assistant and secretary and that was about it. He was left alone by the BBC and Roy Clarke to make the show in his own way.

(864) In the episode In Which Romance Isn't Dead - Just Incompetent, Barry tries to help a man named Chiselhurst in the romance department. Chiselhurst is played by Tyler Butterworth - the son of the great Carry On actor Peter Butterworth.

(865) There are Summer Wine fans who said they stopped watching after Bill Owen died and the Compo funeral episodes ended because they felt the show was never the same. This is fair enough because Bill was such a big part of the show but there were some decent episodes nonetheless post-Compo and the Clegg/Truly/Billy trio wasn't bad once it got going. It is certainly fair to say though that the show struggled, for perfectly understandable and obvious reasons, to recapture past glories once it lost Brian Wilde and Bill

Owen.

(866) Wally Batty has some very elaborate motorcycle leathers for when he gives his bike and sidecar a whirl. It's a wonder he can move in that outfit!

(867) Nicholas Smith was a guest star in the episode titled Will the Genuine Racer Please Stand Up? Smith played Mr Rumbold in Are You Being Served? Sadly though, he doesn't share any scenes in Last of the Summer Wine with his old Are You Being Served? co-star Frank Thornton.

(868) The comedian Brian Conley was a guest star in the 2008 episode Enter the Finger. Conley played Boothroyd, a keep fit fanatic neighbour of Barry - who annoys Barry no end. Russ Abbot was offered this part before it went to Brian Conley. Russ said in an interview that he previously turned down a few guest spots in Summer Wine before he was offered the part of Hobo. The part of Boothroyd was evidently one of them.

(869) A character named Mrs Avery is mentioned a couple of times in Roy Clarke's Open All Hours. Roy obviously decided to recycle this name in Summer Wine.

(870) Bobby Ball's character Lenny is supposed to be some sort of relative to Barry.

(871) In a 1994 interview, Peter Sallis said he wished there were more a few more scenes in Summer Wine of the characters simply having a daft conversation because he felt that comic dialogue was the greatest strength of Roy Clarke as a writer.

(872) In his interviews for Last of the Summer Wine, Brian Murphy always seemed to refer to his character Alvin as 'Elvin'!

(873) There is a slight contradiction between Last of the Summer Wine and First of the Summer Wine when it comes to Clegg's father. Clegg says in Last of the Summer Wine that his father worked on the railways but in the prequel show Clegg's father is a painter and decorator. Maybe we can just pretend he did both?

(874) Ken Kitson and Louis Emerick have done an improvised stage show as the bungling police officers Cooper and Walsh.

(875) When the show was axed, Tom Owen went public in the media and complained about the BBC not commissioning a farewell special. Tom felt the BBC were trying to get rid of Summer Wine as quickly and quietly as they could.

(876) More than one cast member in First of the Summer Wine has since said that Roy Clarke thought Last of the Summer Wine was on its last legs at the time and intended First of the Summer Wine to replace it. Roy slightly contradicted this in interviews as he said he felt it was interesting to have both shows running together so you could dip in and out of the lives of these characters at different ages.

(877) In the stage show they did for Last of the Summer Wine, Peter Sallis and Bill Owen would sometimes break character and talk to the audience - especially if there was a goof or a prop went wrong. It appears that Peter and Jane Freeman didn't think much of the stage show. Jane felt that Last of the Summer Wine didn't work on stage because the outdoor scenes in the Yorkshire hills were such a big part of the appeal and charm of the series.

(878) In the prequel show First of the Summer Wine, Wally is very eager to impress and woo Nora. In decades to come Wally would definitely begin to regret that!

(879) The Suit That Turned Left is one of the rare episodes where Pearl - much to the confusion of Howard - has a radical makeover.

(880) One theory for why First of the Summer Wine never took off was that it ran in conjunction with its parent show. It could be the case that some viewers decided to skip First of the Summer Wine and just watch the 'real thing'. The addition of Peter Sallis to the cast of First of the Summer Wine felt a lot like an attempt to connect it to the base show and perhaps draw a few more viewers in.

(881) One of the brilliant things about Last of the Summer Wine, and one of the keys to its success, was the way that Roy Clarke made the Yorkshire countryside almost like an extra character in the show.

(882) In the one-woman show that Juliette Kaplan did about Pearl, we learn that Pearl was courting a man who then died in the war. This partly explains why Pearl comes to resent Howard. It could be the case that Pearl imagines a more exciting alternative life/reality where she married this other man.

(883) Michael Aldridge said he just used his own voice and accent as Seymour in the end because his attempt to do a Yorkshire accent didn't really work.

(884) Blamire and Foggy had a military background in common so Seymour was something of a departure in that he had an academic background as a teacher.

(885) Alan J W Bell said he didn't enjoy the Last of the Summer Wine stage show very much because he didn't think it was very good. Alan said, in his opinion, the show only came to life when Robert Fyfe and Juliette Kaplan joined the cast as Howard and Pearl.

(886) Robert Fyfe said that he was scared of heights in real life so suffered for his art when Howard has to go on a roof or treehouse in Summer Wine!

(887) There were actually letters of complaint to the BBC show Points of View when Russ Abbot as Hobo made his first appearance in the show. Some long time fans of the show felt that Roy Clarke had lost the plot when Hobo showed up - rambling on about being a spy during the Cold War. To be fair to Roy Clarke and Russ Abbot, Hobo was a work in progress and was improving as a character when the series was axed.

(888) According to some of the cast on First of the Summer Wine, Roy Clarke had a long story arc planned for the show where he would take the characters up to the 1950s and show they how they became the people we see in Last of the Summer Wine. Alas though it wasn't to be as the show was cancelled after two series.

(889) Thora Hird became famous on the Summer Wine set for telling amazing and entertaining stories about her long showbusiness career. The only downside was that in the end the cast felt like they had heard each of these stories about six times!

(890) Given his poor eyesight, it is a wonder Eli doesn't do himself serious harm - especially when he rides a bike!

(891) In the early series of Last of the Summer Wine, Cleggy always seems to have a plastic raincoat.

(892) Dora Bryan won a BAFTA for her performance in the classic 1961 film A Taste of Honey.

(893) The character of Eric Simmonite (played by Barry Hart) appears in the episode Going to Gordon's Wedding and is mentioned (but not seen) in other episodes. It is never made entirely clear what Eric's exact position in the family is or how he is related to Compo.

(894) The Christmas episodes have displayed the best and worst of Auntie Wainwright. She charged 10p for a cup of tea! However, she also laid on a Christmas dinner.

(896) Jane Freeman appeared as the peasant woman Tully Applebottom in the first series of Blackadder (which was called The Black Adder).

(897) Bill Owen played Compo for 27 years in all.

(898) Roy Clarke said that Compo's stunts became more common in Last of the Summer Wine because the physical comedy always got the biggest laughs when a live audience viewed the episodes.

(899) Brian Wilde had a small part in the classic film Night of the Demon. Night of the Demon is a 1957 British horror film directed by Jacques Tourneur and based on the MR James story Casting the Runes.

(900) There is an episode where Cleggy and Truly enjoy some brandy snaps. Brandy snaps are a popular snack or dessert food similar to the Italian cannoli. They are commonly made from a mixture of golden syrup, flour, ginger, cream, sugar, butter and lemon juice.

(901) It is probably fair to say that, although it was a pretty good show, First of the Summer Wine seems to be a trifle forgotten these days.

(902) Peter Sallis said he didn't have to audition for the part of Cleggy. He simply attended an interview with other cast members.

(903) A woman named Sonia Whitehead lived in the house used for Nora's home for many years during Summer Wine. When the BBC were shooting they would replace the door and remove the flowers that Sonia usually had outside. Sonia said that she would often find a gaggle of tourists on her doorstep taking photographs. If that had happened to Nora she'd have taken a broom to them!

(904) Roy Clarke said he had been a fan of Thora Hird for many decades so it was a great honour and pleasure for him when she joined the show as Edie.

(905) Howard's catchphrase is (to Marina of course) - "I think we've really cracked it this time love." Of course, Howard never does crack it. He's always rumbled!

(906) Auntie Wainwright's shop in Summer Wine was a real run down period shop the location scouts found. It was then turned into a house by someone so the Summer Wine production crew had to bolt a shop facade onto the front when they shot the show. You can sometimes see a sign for Garfield Place near the shop. This is a street in Holmfirth.

(907) Jean Alexander said that Danny O'Dea as Eli was the character who always made her laugh the most in the show.

(908) Brian Wilde said that one thing he didn't miss about Summer Wine after he left the show was all that hill walking they had to do!

(909) In the episode Destiny and Six Bananas, Foggy plans to track down giant apes alleged to have been sighted. To this end Foggy has a tranquilliser dart laced with Horlicks! Horlicks is a malted drink which is said to help you sleep.

(910) The postcards being sent to Nora in the episode Support your Local Skydiver are from someone named Gladwin. This is obviously a little nod to the late Joe Gladwin.

(911) Brian Wilde narrated a series of public information films in 1978 which warned children about the dangers of electricity pylons and power stations. Brian played a cartoon owl while a cartoon robin was voiced by Bernard Cribbens.

(912) Billy Hardcastle's favourite film is (no surprise here) The Adventures of Robin Hood with Errol Flynn.

(913) Some of the theme from the film Chariots of Fire can be heard during Compo's training in The Woollenmills of your Mind.

(914) Although he was part of the 'main trio' for a good portion of his tenure, Billy Hardcastle was a bit of a departure for a main trio member because not only was he married he was also clearly younger than the other two (which in this case was obviously Clegg and Truly).

(915) Ken Kitson released a book of poems in 2009. The book is called Moods, Moments & Memories and easy to find on Amazon.

(916) In the documentary which was released to celebrate 25 years of Last of the Summer Wine, Roy Clarke expressed great pride and delight in having Ron Moody in one of the episodes.

(917) You can find a lot of Last of the Summer Wine related merch online these days. Fridge magnets, jigsaw puzzles, calendars, and so forth.

(918) Getting Sam Home was the first episode not to have a laughter track. Roy Clarke later said that Summer Wine didn't feel right unless it had a laughter track - as long as it was genuine live studio audience laughter and not canned laughter. The lack of a laughter track works in Getting Sam Home though because this is for all intents and purposes the big screen Summer Wine feature film we never got.

(919) Malcolm Hebden was a guest star in the 1999 Summer Wine episode The Pony Set. Malcom is a familiar face to British television viewers thanks to his role as Norris Cole in Coronation Street.

(920) Roy Clarke wrote the screenplay for the 1988 drama film Hawks. The story is credited to Barry Gibb - who also supplies the enjoyably dated eighties soundtrack. Hawks is about two terminally ill cancer patients in a London hospital, a lawyer named Bancroft (Timothy Dalton) and a young American football player named Deckermensky (Anthony Edwards), decide to steal an ambulance and head for an Amsterdam brothel for one last adventure before they die. Bancroft believes they are hawks in a world of pigeons and should go out on their own terms rather than ebb away in the ordered confines of a hospital with its rules and conventions. Once in the Netherlands, they meet a pair of mismatched women (played by Camille Coduri and Janet McTeer) who teach them a few lessons about life in a roundabout way. There are Last of the Summer Wine connections in the cast of Hawks because Julie T. Wallace plays a ward sister in the hospital.

(921) Of the location of Holmfirth, Roy Clarke wrote - 'The magic was in the location - in the hills which enclose the town, in the weather swept moors and the valley streams. And it was quiet - self-contained - ignored by the world. Just what we wanted. On our initial look at the place, Jimmy Gilbert - who would produce and direct the show - and I found a community scarcely touched by the times.'

(922) Roy Clarke said that his reservations about Bill Owen playing Compo persisted all through the pre-production because Bill didn't make much of an effort in the read

throughs and rehearsals. It was only when they actually started shooting the show that Bill Owen fully transformed into Compo and Roy Clarke realised he was perfect for the part.

(923) The former Afghan president Hamid Karzai said he was a big fan of Last of the Summer Wine. He said he used to watch it with his son.

(924) The surname of Sid and Ivy was never revealed in the show.

(925) The satirical comic Viz once had a spoof Last of the Summer Wine story called Last of the Armageddon Wine. In the story, Compo, Clegg, and Foggy make a nuclear bomb!

(926) Bill Owen was in a lot of films as a younger man but his hopes of being a leading man were dashed by the fact that he was only 5'4.

(927) It is noticeable that in Magic And The Morris Minor, the last episode Bill Owen appeared in, that Compo is absent from some of the interior scenes.

(928) The episode Spring Fever indicates that Compo is a fan of mushy peas.

(929) Last of the Summer Wine was shown on various PBS stations in the United States.

(930) Peter Sallis used to work in a bank before he became an actor. He also had a spell serving in the RAF.

(931) They had to age Jean Alexander up with makeup to play Auntie Wainwright. Jean looked much younger than the character in real life.

(932) Jane Freeman's first television role was in the 1964 series Diary of a Young Man. Jane was cast by the director Ken Loach. Only a few episodes of this series remain today as half of them were lost. In those days they used to 'wipe' television shows by taping new shows over them. It obviously didn't occur to television companies at the time that people in the future would be interested in watching old shows from the past.

(933) The name of Lynda Baron's character in Getting Sam Home is Lily Bless'er.

(934) In reality, Sid and Ivy's cafe is probably a bit on the small side to make much of a profit. You can't fit many customers in there - though it rarely seems very busy.

(935) Auntie Wainwright is pretty ruthless when it comes to finding customers. Even if you so much as walk past her shop she'll consider you fair game and find some ruse to get you inside!

(936) The burly fellow who takes Foggy outside in The Man From Oswestry is Compo's cousin Big Malcolm Simmonite. Malcom was played by Paul Luty. Paul Luty was a wrestler before he became an actor. The character of Big Malcolm Simmonite only appeared in one episode. It seems as if Roy Clarke created this big extended family for Compo to come in and out of the show in guest spots but then thought better of the idea and got rid of it in the end.

(937) A big difference between Blamire and Clegg and Compo is that Blamire doesn't like not having a job. Clegg and Compo on the other hand can get by quite happily without employment.

(938) In the early episode Pate and Chips, we meet another of Compo's relatives - Chip Simmonite (played by Tony

Haygarth). Chip is married to Connie (Margaret Nolan). Chip and Connie are quite unusual for Summer Wine characters because they have kids and a happy marriage! These characters did not return though in the future.

(939) In the 1998 episode Nowhere Particular, Cleggy and Truly only appear in a couple of scenes. The show was clearly becoming more of an ensemble by now.

(940) Peter Sallis achieved international recognition as the voice of Wallace, the eccentric inventor and cheese lover, in the animated films created by Aardman Animations.

(941) In a 2016 interview, Roy Clarke suggested that it is more difficult to write comedy today. "Whatever you say these days you upset somebody. It is not like the old days. Now they feel entitled to be upset. I think we have lost all common sense."

(942) The pilot for the proposed Cooper and Walsh spin-off show was much as you'd expect - with the two coppers sitting in their car in some rural spot having a daft conversation. Apparently, had a full series gone ahead, they were open to actors from Last of the Summer Wine making guest appearances in Cooper and Walsh. Despite the participation of Alan J W Bell and Roy Clarke, funding for Cooper and Walsh failed to transpire though and so the show didn't go ahead.

(943) Russ Abbot is plainly wearing a toupee as Hobo.

(944) Clegg visits the grave of his late wife Edith in the pilot episode but we never see him do this again in the show. We would have to presume though that Clegg does go there from time to time when he isn't with the others.

(945) The proximity of locations in Summer Wine, like the cafe, character homes, and the countryside, are not as near

together in real life as the show implies.

(946) Foggy Dewhurst claims to be a master of the martial arts and deadly in unarmed combat. Suffice to say, Foggy never actually provides any evidence for this in the show.

(947) Eli's cameos in Last of the Summer Wine are very self-contained and usually have no relevance to the plots. They are just fun little comic interludes which occur at random.

(948) Peter Sallis said he nearly drowned shooting a water sequence in Ballad for Wind Instruments and Canoe. Some of the things that actors did in the old sitcoms definitely wouldn't be allowed today.

(949) First of the Summer Wine has a laughter track - like the parent show. The laughter track doesn't really suit First of the Summer Wine though for some reason. You don't really notice the laughter track in Last of the Summer Wine but in First of the Summer Wine it feels slightly obtrusive.

(950) Kathy Staff said she nearly missed out on playing Nora because she was initially deemed too slim to play the character.

(951) David Fenwick played Cleggy in First of the Summer Wine. David's first television role was as a drug pusher in Grange Hill!

(952) Tom Simmonite moved into Compo's old house for a time and Mrs Avery developed something of a rivalry with Nora over cleaning and whether Tom was getting enough grub. Roy Clarke pulled the plug on this set-up fairly quickly as it was going nowhere in particular.

(953) Compo is clearly a man who can handle his drink. He can down a pint in one and is always ready for another.

However, even Compo was the worse for wear after drinking a mite too much home brew at Ernie Mordew's funeral tea in The Black Widow. This is a classic episode where Cleggy finds himself at the mercy of Mrs Jack Attercliffe.

(954) Foggy is always complaining that Compo and Cleggy are in bad shape and should get fitter. However, whenever he does something strenuous we see that an exhausted Foggy isn't exactly Daley Thompson himself!

(955) Smiler got so sick of being Nora Batty's lodger that in the end he offered £50 to anyone who would get him thrown out!

(956) The reason why Michael Bates still appeared in It Ain't Half Hot Mum after leaving Last of the Summer Wine for health reasons is that his role in It Ain't Half Hot Mum was studio based. Michael could still do some stuff in a studio but Last of the Summer Wine was more taxing because it required a lot of outdoor location work.

(957) The reason why there was no series of Last of the Summer Wine in 1978 and only Christmas specials is that Roy Clarke was busy with Open All Hours and Peter Sallis was appearing in a (now completely forgotten) sitcom called Leave it to Charlie.

(958) In a 2022 interview, Les Dennis (who worked with Russ Abbot on Russ's old comedy sketch shows) said that Russ was disillusioned by the fact that The Russ Abbot Show (which had millions of viewers in the 1980s) is never repeated anywhere now and has been a bit forgotten. If it is any consolation to Russ, he can rest assured that Last of the Summer Wine repeats are very common!

(959) In relation to the large cast and guest stars, Peter Sallis once said that Last of the Summer Wine was like National Service in that literally everyone had to do it in the end!

Warren Mitchell has also been credited with this quote.

(960) The reason why giving Compo a large extended family in the early series of Summer Wine doesn't quite work is that the main trio being disconnected - save for each other - gives them a sort of outsider status which adds a bittersweet quality to their friendship.

(961) The episode Isometrics and After was the last one which featured the library in the early run of the show. Many years later the library would return with Miss Davenport in charge.

(962) Given all the elaborate experiments and stunts that Foggy and Seymour subject Compo to, you sometimes wonder if they aren't trying to murder him!

(963) The main cast of First of the Summer Wine were mostly in their early twenties when they made the show and staying together in a hotel and having fun. Apparently, they would often turn up for shooting in the morning a little the worse for wear after a late night of partying!

(964) After her introduction as Edie in Uncle of the Bride, Thora Hird appeared in all but ten episodes until her death in 2003.

(965) Series nine was an unusually long one for Last of the Summer Wine as it ran to twelve episodes.

(966) Although he was a linoleum salesman, Cleggy says in Last of the Summer Wine that he doesn't even like lino!

(967) In real life, Juliette Kaplan's mother was named Pearl. Juliette said it was a rather spooky and strange coincidence that her most famous role saw her playing a character with the same name as her mother.

(968) Roy Clarke said he found the character of Seymour more difficult to write for than Foggy. Roy said it took a while to get a grip on how to write Seymour.

(969) The backstory of Herbert Truelove is obviously that he grew up with Cleggy and Compo but then moved to London and later become a police officer. Truly moves back to Yorkshire when he retires - and is reunited with Cleggy and Compo again.

(970) One of the main reasons why Robert Fyfe was asked to join the television show is that he proved to have good comic chemistry with Peter Sallis in the Last of the Summer Wine stage show. The exchanges between Cleggy and Howard in the stage show were very amusing.

(971) Thora Hird was seventy-four years-old when she was cast as Edie in Last of the Summer Wine.

(972) Tom Owen said there was a strange and emotional atmosphere on the set of Last of the Summer Wine when he joined the cast. The other actors were still finding it sad and surreal to shoot new episodes without the late Bill Owen.

(973) Although she'd been in Last of the Summer Wine as Pearl for years at the time, Juliette Kaplan said she only met Roy Clarke for the first time in 2003!

(974) Louis Emerick made his debut as PC Walsh in the episode Downhill Racer. This was five months before Louis was cast as Mick Johnson in Brookside - which explains why PC Walsh left Summer Wine for quite a time soon afterwards.

(975) Sticky buns have been consumed since the Middle Ages.

(976) Mike Grady was no stranger to sitcoms before Summer Wine because he played the character Ken in Citizen Smith.

Citizen Smith aired from 1977 to 1980. The show was created by John Sullivan. The main character is Wolfie Smith, played by Robert Lindsay. Wolfie is a young socialist revolutionary who believes in creating a workers' republic in Britain. He is often seen wearing a Che Guevara-style beret and leading protests against the capitalist system. However, his plans are often comically foiled by his lack of organisational skills and the general apathy of his fellow citizens.

(977) In the original plan for Last of the Summer Wine the main trio were going to be in their 70s. The producer and director James Gilbert decided though that the three main characters should be a bit younger than this. This was an important change because rather than be long retired the characters were now redundant or suddenly retired at an age when they are still capable of working.

(978) Jean Alexander was what you could describe as a true character actor. As Jean would always point out, in real life she was nothing like Hilda Ogden or Auntie Wainwright!

(979) Jean Fergusson said she was frequently covered in mud and leaves making Last of the Summer Wine because Marina usually ends hiding in a hedge in many episodes!

(980) Compo's old house has clearly been decorated by the time Alvin moves in. Not before time you might say!

(981) Kathy Staff was born Minnie Higginbottom.

(982) Last of the Summer Wine was said to be the favourite show of the late Queen Elizabeth II.

(983) The Yorkshire poet Ian McMillan said of Last of the Summer Wine - "For me the language was always the glory. Roy Clarke sat in that windmill near Doncaster and he came up with some amazing lines; about really deep things and love and despair."

(984) Getting Sam Home rather anticipates the film Weekend at Bernie's! Weekend at Bernie's is a 1989 comedy film directed by Ted Kotcheff. The movie follows the misadventures of two young office workers, Larry and Richard, who discover that their boss, Bernie Lomax, has been embezzling money from their company. However, when they confront Bernie about it, they accidentally discover that he is dead. Rather than reporting the death to the police, Larry and Richard decide to pretend that Bernie is still alive, as they fear that they will be blamed for the embezzlement if his death is discovered. Throughout the weekend, they go to great lengths to make it appear that Bernie is alive, creating humorous and absurd situations along the way.

(985) The young cast in First of the Summer Wine are today older than Peter Sallis and Brian Wilde were when they first started playing Cleggy and Foggy in Last of the Summer Wine!

(986) Apart from Crusher and Babs, Last of the Summer Wine never really experimented with introducing a young character as a regular. In fact, when you watch Last of the Summer Wine it is often as if the characters live in a world where there are no young people!

(987) Roy Clarke said a key to the longevity of Last of the Summer Wine is that the BBC left them alone and didn't meddle with the scripts or the show.

(988) Billy Hardcastle ended up living next to Truly in the show.

(989) There was apparently a bit of a battle between Alan J W Bell and Sydney Lotterby over who would get to direct Getting Sam Home. Alan was determined to do it because it was his idea to do a feature length film in the first place.

(990) Whoops and Getting Sam Home both feature lyrics with the theme tune. Many years later, Just a Small Funeral also used the lyrics.

(991) Roy Clarke was awarded an OBE in 2002. Roy said that when he got his OBE from Prince Charles (as he was back then), Prince Charles told him that he loved Last of the Summer Wine.

(992) A BBC poll in 2006 ranked Last of the Summer Wine as the fourteenth best British sitcom of all time. Roy Clarke's other two most famous sitcoms actually finished higher. Open All Hours was eighth and Keeping Up Appearances was eleventh.

(993) Duncan Wood is a pivotal figure in the story of Last of the Summer because it was Wood who approached Roy Clarke with the general idea in the first place. Duncan Wood was a comedy producer, director and writer. He produced all of Tony Hancock's Half Hours during the late 1950s and early 1960s, and later, also with Hancock's former writers Ray Galton and Alan Simpson, the sitcom Steptoe and Son for most of its run. From 1970 to 1973, he was the BBC's Head of Comedy.

(994) Peter Sallis was actually building up quite a fun horror CV before he became best known for Last of the Summer Wine. Peter was in The Curse of the Werewolf, Taste the Blood of Dracula, Scream and Scream Again, and Frankenstein: The True Story.

(995) I Was A Hitman For Primrose Dairies was a sort of soft reboot for the show because it introduced Hobo and Stella, had a new main trio, and reduced Cleggy and Truly to very minor supporting characters (which was obviously unavoidable due to the age of Peter Sallis and Frank Thornton).

(996) Last of the Summer Wine was a trifle more gritty and abrasive in the early series compared to the 'gentle' and cosy show it became in the end. Roy Clarke said that making Summer Wine more gentle and family friendly was definitely deliberate.

(997) Bert Parnaby made two appearances in Summer Wine as Jack Harry Teasdale. Jack is a shopkeeper and friend of the main trio.

(998) Wally Batty is a pigeon fancier and finds solace and contentment when he visits his pigeon loft. Wally especially enjoys watching a pigeon fly off to freedom because this is something he desperately yearns to do himself!

(999) Kathy Staff wore two sets of padding to bulk her up as the beefy Nora Batty. Kathy actually wore an oversized man's vest to keep the padding in place.

(1000) Roy Clarke has said that he misses writing Last of the Summer Wine because it was such a big part of his life. Those characters almost felt real to him in the end.

Milton Keynes UK
Ingram Content Group UK Ltd.
UKHW010022030424
440481UK00001B/131

9 798223 398240